Iain Banks's
Complicity

D1458469

CONTINUUM CONTEMPORARIES

Also available in this series:

Pat Barker's *Regeneration*, by Karin Westman
Kazuo Ishiguro's *The Remains of the Day*, by Adam Parkes
Carol Shields's *The Stone Diaries*, by Abby Werlock
J. K. Rowling's *Harry Potter Novels*, by Philip Nel
Jane Smiley's *A Thousand Acres*, by Susan Farrell
Barbara Kingsolver's *The Poisonwood Bible*, by Linda Wagner-Martin
Irvine Welsh's *Trainspotting*, by Robert Morace
Donna Tartt's *The Secret History*, by Tracy Hargreaves
Toni Morrison's *Paradise*, by Kelly Reames
Don DeLillo's *Underworld*, by John Duvall
Annie Proulx's *The Shipping News*, by Aliki Varvogli
Graham Swift's *Last Orders*, by Pamela Cooper
Haruki Murakami's *The Wind-up Bird Chronicle*, by Matthew Strecher
Ian Rankin's *Black and Blue*, by Gill Plain
Bret Easton Ellis's *American Psycho*, by Julian Murphet
Cormac McCarthy's *All the Pretty Horses*, by Stephen Tatum
Michael Ondaatje's *The English Patient*, by John Bolland
A.S. Byatt's *Possession*, by Catherine Burgass
David Guterson's *Snow Falling on Cedars*, by Jennifer Haytock
Helen Fielding's *Bridget Jones's Diary*, by Imelda Whelehan
Sebastian Faulks's *Birdsong*, by Pat Wheeler
Kate Atkinson's *Behind the Scenes at the Museum*, by Emma Parker
Hanif Kureishi's *The Buddha of Suburbia*, by Nahem Yousaf
Nick Hornby's *High Fidelity*, by Joanne Knowles
Zadie Smith's *White Teeth*, by Claire Squires
Arundhati Roy's *The God of Small Things*, by Julie Mullaney
Alan Warner's *Morvern Callar*, by Sophy Dale
Margaret Atwood's *Alias Grace*, by Gina Wisker
Vikram Seth's *A Suitable Boy*, by Angela Atkins

Forthcoming in this series:

Jonathan Coe's *What a Carve Up!*, by Pamela Thurschwell
Louis De Bernieres's *Captain Corelli's Mandolin*, by Con Coroneos

· IAIN BANKS'S

Complicity

A READER'S GUIDE

CAIRNS CRAIG

CONTINUUM | NEW YORK | LONDON

2002

The Continuum International Publishing Group Inc
370 Lexington Avenue, New York, NY 10017

The Continuum International Publishing Group Ltd
The Tower Building, 11 York Road, London SE1 7NX

www.continuumbooks.com

Copyright © 2002 by Cairns Craig

Printed in the United States of America

Library of Congress Cataloging-in-Publication Data
Library of Congress Cataloging-in-Publication Data

Craig, Cairns.
    Iain Banks's Complicity : a reader's guide / Cairns Craig.
        p. cm. — (Continuum contemporaries)
    Includes bibliographical references (p.   ).
    ISBN 0-8264-5247-7 (alk. paper)
    1. Banks, Iain. Complicity.   I. Title.   II. Series.

PR6052.A485 C583 2002
823'.914—dc21

                                                    2001053913

ISBN 0-8264-5247-7

Contents

The Novelist

Iain Banks leapt to fame — or, perhaps more accurately, to notoriety — in 1984 with his first published novel, *The Wasp Factory*. Born in Dunfermline, Fife on 16 February 1954, Banks had left Stirling University with an Ordinary Degree in 1975 and had spent ten years doing a variety of jobs — from technician at the Nigg Bay oil platform construction site, and in the IBM computer plant at Gourock, to clerk in a law firm in London — during which he had also written at least seven novels. His science fiction novel, *The Player of Games*, had almost been accepted a year before the *The Wasp Factory* but that book, he claimed, was the first book he had properly revised. It is the story of teenager Frank Cauldhame (Scots for "cold home"), who claims to have murdered his brother Paul and two of his cousins. Frank lives alone with his father, a scientist and former hippy, in a house in which each maintains his room locked against the other. They live in expectation and in fear of the return home of his other, mad, half-brother, Eric, who has escaped from a mental hospital and whose particular passion is for the brutal maiming and killing of dogs. Frank himself has been mauled by a dog which, he believes, castrated him when he was small.

The savage violence of *The Wasp Factory*, and its casual attitude to murder, ensured that it got lots of attention but it made many reviewers uncertain — indeed, deeply ambivalent — about how to respond to Banks's writing. The *Irish Times* declared that "it is a sick, sick world when the confidence and investment of an astute firm of publishers is justified by a work of unparalleled depravity", and even those who wanted to declare it a "minor masterpiece" (*Punch*) felt that there was "something foreign and nasty" in it, perhaps associated with the Scottish origins stressed by the *Sunday Express*, which described it as "a silly, gloatingly sadistic and grisly yarn of a family of Scots lunatics". The plot's conclusion in which the narrator, Frank, is discovered *not* to be a castrated boy but a girl, Frances, whose bodily development has been repressed by chemicals fed to her by her father, led reviewers into seeing Banks as endowed with, or suffering from, a "bizarre fertility" and a "repellent inventiveness"; he had produced "an obsessive novel, a bad dream of a book". The *Times Literary Supplement* was confident that Banks's writing was dictated by market forces, and that he had decided that "the surest way to make an impact with a first novel, if not the most satisfactory, is to deal in extremes of oddity and unpleasantness: so in *The Wasp Factory* we have some ghoulish frivolity and a good deal of preposterous sadism".

It is symptomatic of the disjunction between reviewers' fears for their readers — "If you are squeamish or easily frightened, then leave *The Wasp Factory* severely alone", the *Daily Express* warned — and publishers' conceptions of what attracts readers' interest that all of the above quotes appear in the preliminary pages of the paperback edition of *The Wasp Factory*, published six years after the original hardback. By that time, the dubious reviews had become an accolade and Banks had become a phenomenon — a writer who could sell in vast quantities to a popular and mostly youthful audience and yet who, despite the outrageous violence of some of his plots, could also command serious critical attention. Moreover, he led a barely concealed double life by publishing (under what can only be described as the "*non*-de-plume" of Iain M. Banks) a series of science fiction novels which would rapidly establish him as Britain's most challenging writer in that genre. A writer of fiction in a "popular" genre, like science fiction, who could also command a popular audience for his "serious" novels; a Scottish writer who could command a British audience for novels about Scotland; a writer who could appeal to a youth audience (knowledgeable about the popular culture of music and drugs) and an audience of serious academic scholars, Banks was in a category all of his own.

Youthful readers of Banks's first novel may have grasped its mode better than his serious reviewers, perhaps because it mixes high and low culture in the manner of *Monty Python's Flying Circus*, a scene from which is parodied when Frank is attacked by a killer rabbit. Like the best sketches from *Python*, Banks's novel is built on a series of parodies of modern culture's primal myths. Frank is a *Frank*enstein, created by his mad scientist father, but instead of a male monster imagined by a female author (Mary Shelley), Frank-in-Frances is a female "monster" imagined by a male author. And instead of the tragic tale of the monster being driven out of society into the wilderness, Frank is allowed to return to society — as Frances — by the kind of sexual reversion, re-establishing the possibility of natural harmony and vitality, used in Shakespearean comedies such as *Twelfth Night*.

Banks studied Philosophy and Psychology, as well as English Literature, at Stirling University, and Frank is also constructed as a parody of Freudian psychology, and, in particular, of Freud's conception that women suffer from a castration complex. In the context of Freudian psychology female identity depends not on positive attributes (having a vagina) but on negatives — the lack of a penis. Banks actualizes Freud's psychology by having Frances believe she is a castrated "Frank". At the same time, he turns the Freudian version of sexuality inside-out by endowing his (concealed) female protagonist with the aggression and violence usually associated only with masculinity. The transfer of "normal" gender attributes from male to female undermines conventional notions of masculinity and femininity, emphasizing that they are socially constructed rather than biological categories.

The Wasp Factory delineates a terrain which will be typical of Banks's later novels, in that Frank's life is lived in the aftermath of apocalyptic events, both personal and historical. Not only does "he" live in the aftermath of "his" castration but he also inhabits a psychological landscape that is the inner equivalent of the apocalyptic novels of the period after the World War II, such as William Golding's *Lord of the Flies*. Frank's personal world—he prepares heads for his "Sacrifice Poles" in "the Bunker"—is a grim mirror-image of the world that twentieth-century history has bequeathed to those born after Hitler's death in his Bunker, and Frank's campaign to make himself "unchallenged lord of the island and the lands about it" (p. 139) both mimics the violence of the first half of the twentieth century and, at the same time, asserts "his" desire to escape from that world into one that is under his own control.

The Wasp Factory establishes four major issues that Banks would explore in later novels: (1) war and peace, (2) sexual transgression, (3) the rules of the game, (4) subverting genre.

WAR AND PEACE

Banks's father worked in the admiralty. Till the age of nine, he lived in North Queensferry, close to the Rosyth dockyards where naval ships are refitted and, thereafter, in Gourock, on the Firth of Clyde, close to where both the American and British nuclear submarine fleets were based. The years when Banks was attending secondary school in Gourock were the years of the Vietnam War and the international Peace Movement. War, real and imagined, is the background against which all of his characters develop, attempting to understand the relationship between the virtues of peaceful civilization and the violence on which it seems to be based. Banks's characters are caught in a world that makes it impossible for them to tell whether they are committed to violence in order to attain peace or committed to peace only as a justification for their violence. Frank, for instance, wards off invasions of his island — and maintains its peace — by the effect of his "Sacrifice Poles". The Sacrifice Poles, however, require heads mounted on them and so demand that he has to kill things: "How the hell am I supposed to get heads and bodies for the Poles and the Bunker if I don't kill things?" he asks; "There just aren't enough natural deaths. You can't explain that sort of thing to people, though" (p. 13). The presumed normality of his violence is juxtaposed with his Father's "hippy-anarchist" (p. 14) retreat from the world to their island sanctuary, as though the peaceful intentions of the 1960s generation of "flower-power" is eternally haunted by the demonic violence which it sought to deny.

Similarly, in Banks's second novel, *Walking on Glass*, one of the characters, Steven Grout, believes himself to be exiled from a greater reality, one where war makes life significant compared to the insignificance of his life in late-twentieth century London:

There was a war somewhere. He didn't know where. Not a place you could necessarily get to by travelling anywhere from here, late Twentieth Century London, Earth, but somewhere, sometime. It was the ultimate war, the final confrontation between Good and Evil, and he had played a major part in the war. But something had gone wrong, he had been betrayed, lost a battle with forces of chaos and been ejected from the real battleground to languish here, in this cesspit they called 'life'. (p. 26)

The peaceful but banal world of the modern city breeds a deep nostalgia for the moral significance given to life by war. The confrontation between elemental war and peace are also played out in Iain M. Banks's science fiction novels, in which the Culture, a fundamentally peaceful and democratic civilization of the distant future, has to defend itself against the violence of other civilizations that have power and domination as their aims. In *The Player of Games* (1988), Gurgeh, the Culture's highest-ranking player of intellectual games, finds himself pitted against the Emperor of the civilization of Azad in a game that imitates war but which, it turns out, is being played for real. To defend himself and the Culture of which he is part, Gurgeh has to become his own opposite, has to acquire the warrior virtues from which his civilization should protect him: "So now the man played like one of those carnivores he'd been listening to, stalking across the board, setting up traps and diversions and killing grounds; pouncing, pursuing, bringing down, consuming, absorbing . . ." (p. 247). The transformation of the civilized into the violent is also the theme of *Canal Dreams*, the novel which has always come last both in Banks's own and his readers' estimation, but which powerfully explores the aftermath of war and its relationship to peace through the culture which has been most traumatically involved in both — Japan. The protagonist, Hisako Onada, is a middle-aged Japanese cellist, daughter of one of those who died as a consequence of the Hiroshima bombing, who has, like the defeated culture of which she is the inheritor, adopted Western values in both art and politics. However, her commitment to the beauties of music in a peaceful world conceal the fact that — like so many of Banks's protagonists — she has been responsible for a terrible act of violence, in this case the death of a policeman during a student protest rally. The peaceful world of culture towards which she strives is constantly undermined by the violent, war-torn history in which she is caught up, and, like many of Banks's characters, she finds herself driven to extremes of violence in order to preserve the possibility of a culture of peace.

In the aftermath of the World War II, Scotland was an apparently peaceful country. Compulsory military service was abandoned by the British government in the late 1950s and Scotland's military involvements were in distant Cold War conflicts such as Korea or end-of-Empire retreats such as Suez and Cyprus. Despite this, Scotland was an armed arsenal, a front-line battleship of the Cold War, providing a European base for the U.S. nuclear threat to Russia. Scotland, it was often claimed, contained the largest concentration of war weaponry anywhere in the Free World. Frank Cauldhame's home in *The Wasp Factory* might be an image of Scotland itself, since it sits on a cellar where an unstable arsenal of cordite left over from the World War II is stored, representing, according to Frank, some "link with the past, or an evil demon we have lurking, a symbol for all our family misdeeds; waiting, perhaps, one day to surprise us" (p. 53). In Banks's novels, the violence of the past is always waiting, in one form or another, to return to us. Not for nothing is the ship on which Hisako Onada is trapped in *Canal Dreams* called *Le Cercle*: the past which we seek to put behind us is, for Banks, always going to circle back in a new and even more violent form.

The relationship between culture and violence is often dramatized in Banks's novels in the image of the castle. Banks's concern with the symbol of the castle is widely acknowledged and he has said himself that he is sees it as an image of the self. Internally, it represents a secure space within which culture can be protected, where personal relations and aesthetic appreciation can flourish but, externally, it is built as a strategic emplacement in the business of war and conquest. Culture can flourish only within the secure ramparts that deflect the violence of the outside world, and can survive only by being prepared to assert itself by the violent means to which it seems, at first sight, entirely opposed. It is a theme that Banks works out at its most extreme in *A Song of Stone*, a much underrated and misunderstood novel.

The protagonist of *A Song of Stone*, Abel, is the inheritor of a castle in an unnamed country and at an unstated time in history. It represents the center of all wars: "I do not understand their war, nor know who fights nor for what and why. This could be any place or time, and any cause could bring the same results, the same ends, loose or met, or won or lost" (p. 272). The castle and its grounds have sheltered his delicate and aesthetic existence, where he is set aside from ordinary life: "to be worth anything at all I—we—must evade such mundane pursuits and set ourselves apart as much in the staging of that customary act as in our dress, habitation, speech or subsidiary manners" (p. 71). But in war the castle will suddenly be returned to its original purpose: a place of defense, a place of aggression, a place in which all the fine things of civilization are brought to nothing. "I think now I may have been shortsighted", Abel muses, "not to have realised that though we live in periods of peace they are as much the store of just their opposite as accumulations of wealth, two-faced, implies impoverishment in its gift" (p. 229). War aims at achieving peace, but the peace it produces becomes, in Banks's fiction, simply the storehouse of another war. Civilization, in the end, has to defend itself through barbarity: "I thought, through a display of civility, to show my contempt for these desperate days and our lieutenant's brash assumptions, but forced beyond a certain point, such politeness becomes self-defeating. I must allow myself to be infected by the violent nature of the times" (p. 247). It is our inevitable complicity with the "violent nature of the times", the time defined between the Falklands War of 1982 and the Gulf War of 1991, that Banks explores in *Complicity*.

SEXUAL TRANSGRESSION

In *The Wasp Factory* Frank's violence is linked directly to his belief
in his own violent castration and its "unmanning" of him:

Having no purpose in life or procreation, I invested all my worth in that
grim opposite, and so found a negative and negation of the fecundity only
others could lay claim to. I believe that I decided if I could never become
a man, I—the unmanned—would out-man those around me, and so I
became the killer, a small image of the ruthless soldier-hero almost all I've
ever seen or read seems to pay strict homage to. (p. 183)

Frances, of course, is making an even greater transformation of
herself when she becomes the "the ruthless soldier-hero", since
the feminine is having to shape itself to the expectations of masculine identity. Frances's adaptation of herself to the most violent
version of masculinity is repeated in both *Canal Dreams* and in
A Song of Stone. In the former, Hisako Onada transforms herself
from into a figure of violent vengefulness, slaughtering those who
have raped her; in the latter, the soldiers who take over the Castle
are led by a female lieutenant who has no compunction about
ordering less adroit looters than herself to be hanged from the
castle walls.

Such inversions of gender characteristics have regularly been
used by Banks to explore the nature of masculinity through the eyes
of female narrators—Frances in *The Wasp Factory*, Isis in *Whit*,
Kathryn Telman in *The Business*—or female protagonists—Hisako
Onada in *Canal Dreams*—who, by their ability to take on male
characteristics, reveal the social conventions by which masculinity
is constructed and the will to power which it expresses. Many of
these female characters grow through their adoption of maleness

into something incorporating or transcending both. In Banks's novels, gender is not destiny but a social convention which can be transferred between the sexes. Any character, therefore, can be like the conception of God promulgated by the religious cult to which Isis belongs in *Whit*, since God is "both and neither male and female, and everything else as well" (p. 52). Frank in *The Wasp Factory* rediscovering him/herself to be Frances is only one of Banks's many gender inversions, inversions that become, in his science fiction works, a part of the alternative reality of the future in which individuals can physically change gender in the course of their lives, or in which there are a variety of different genders. Alternative forms of sexual expression or sexual partnership are no less evident in Banks's "realistic" novels. Abel, in *A Song of Stone*, for instance, makes love to the earth itself: "I started to strip off my soaking clothes, wriggling wetly from them, casting them aside, half-maddened, half incited by their cloying, clinging resistance, until finally I was naked in the cold filth, rolling in it like a dog in ordure, freezing and numb but laughing and growling, smoothing that slime all over my body, excited by its clammy caress so that the cold and wet fought a losing battle with my own raised heat" (p. 54). Isis, in *Whit*, on the other hand, is preparing herself for a union of a transcendent kind in a "Festival of Love in all its forms, including the holy communing of souls through the blessed glory of sexual congress" (p. 200).

In Banks's novels, sexuality acts as the primary focus of society's constructions of rules, both about individual conduct and about gender identity. The plots of many of his novels revolve around sexual acts that transgress "normal" or traditional sexual conventions. Thus in *Whit*, Salvador confers upon himself the right to perform his own marriage ceremony and to marry himself to two sisters at the same time, "normalizing" bigamy within the rules of his own religion. Equally, as Isis grows to maturity, he decides that sexual congress between grandfather and granddaughter is also within the rules:

He raised his head and brought his face up to mine. "We must join our souls, child. We must commune together!" He pushed his mouth towards mine.

"What?" I yelped, bringing my arms up to his shoulders to try to push him away. "But, Grandfather!"

"I know!" he cried hoarsely, as his head turned this way and that, trying to bring our lips together. "I know it seems wrong, but I hear Their voice!"

"But it's forbidden!" I said, straining at his shoulders, still trying to push him back. He was forcing me over and down now, onto the bed beneath. "We are two generations apart!"

"It was forbidden; but it isn't any more. That was a mistake. The Voice was clear about that". (p. 276)

Salvador's defiance of the taboo on inter-familial sex is part of his belief in "free love" but he is typical of Banks's concern with characters who believe themselves to be able to define their own morality. In Isis's case, her Grandfather declares that "This is meant. We are the elect; the chosen ones. The rules are different for us"; being the elect they "don't have to take any notice of the Unsaved's stupid rules" (p. 277). A similar refusal of the rules is the basis of the central relationship in *A Song of Stone*, in which Abel refuses to conform to "outmoded morality" in order to continue a "close but prohibited union" (p. 232). In this case, the very fact of interfamilial sex makes the characters special, transforming them into an elect who can refuse the banal rules of sex: "to be worth anything at all I — we — must evade such mundane pursuits and set ourselves apart as much in the staging of that customary act as in our dress, habitation, speech or subsidiary manners" (p. 71). When the castle is taken over by a group of rebel soldiers, however, gender expectations are given a further twist. The leader of the soldiers is a female lieutenant who takes the protagonist's partner—Morgan (note the androgynous name)—from him. Playing a male role in leading her men—a commandeered piece of artillery is christened "The Lieutenant's Prick" (p. 175)—the lieutenant engages Morgan in a lesbian relationship and the protagonist is displaced by a woman better capable than him of playing a man's role. The reversal of their roles is metaphorically enacted at the novel's conclusion when, after the lieutenant's death, Abel is strung up on the gun, on the "Lieutenant's Prick", to await execution.

That concluding image in *A Song of Stone* reveals the relationship of socially constructed notions of masculinity to violence that is central to Banks's writing. Banks's skill in detailing technology—whether real technology or the fantasy technologies of his science fiction—and his eye for the fashions of technological gadgets is one of the delights of his novels, but the technologies are often the expression of a masculinist ideology which is fundamentally self-destructive. Within a definition of "maleness" that is focused on notions of the "ruthless soldier-hero", or aggressively acquisitive materialism, or sexual domination, technology becomes the tool by which the world is subdued, but subdued only by being distorted and, in the end, wrecked. The wrecked landscapes that litter Banks's novels are the outcome of an ideology of power and oppression within which masculinity has been defined. For Banks, sexual transgression can be simply another form of the will to power, of the individual's assertion of himself—or herself—on the world, or it can be the opening up of alternative forms of sexual identity that will help us escape the wreckage of the past. The difficult is in knowing which is which, and the intertwining of sexual liberation, sexual repression and violence is a major theme of *Complicity*.

THE RULES OF THE GAME

The rules that surround sexuality emphasize that human beings are, for Banks, in all of their activities, players of games. As Gurgeh, protagonist of the novel of that name announces, games are crucial to human beings not just because we learn to be human through our childhood games but because games are human versions of reality itself:

All reality is a game. Physics at its most fundamental, the very fabric of our universe, results directly from the interaction of certain fairly simple rules, and chance; the same description may be applied to the best, most elegant and both intellectually and aesthetically satisfying games. (p. 41)

A game is the universe in miniature and the societies in which we live are nothing but complicated games that we learn to play for real. Thus in *Whit*, Isis discovers that when she leaves the enclosed world of her spiritual community, with its own particular rules and prohibitions, she has to negotiate her way through the very different structures of the world outside, trying to fit her rules to its require-ments: "We are not averse to travelling in trains — either sitting on the floor of the guard's van or using the wooden Sitting Boards we carry to avoid the luxury of soft furnishings — but my mission was so important I had to be rigorous in my piety, and there was something too beguilingly easy about simply avoiding paying my fare on an ordinary passenger train" (p. 84). The various rules and prohibitions of Isis's religion form a game at which she has become an expert player, just as, for Abel in *A Song of Stone*, those involved in any political or social action are protagonists in a game, despite the fact that the outcome is a matter of life and death: "There are tensions between states, peoples, races, castes and classes which any given player—individual or group—simply neglects, takes for granted or attempts to manipulate for their advantage only at the risk of their very existence" (p. 78).

Games, in Banks's work, continually turn from playful, self-contained analogues of reality into reality itself. Equally, the "reality" in which human beings believe themselves to be acting turns out to be a "game" played to someone else's rules, which is why many of Banks's novels turn on the discovery of a complicated "plot" that one character has fabricated and in which another is trapped. In *The Crow Road*, for instance, Prentice McHoan has to unravel the plots of his Uncle Fergus in order to discover what has happened to his other, missing, Uncle Rory—just as Isis, in *Whit*, has to uncover her brother Allan's plot to take over the community. For each protagonist, what they took to be "reality"—Frank's castration in *The Wasp Factory*—turns out to be a game invented and imposed on them by someone else. For many of Banks's characters, the solution to the discovery that they have been trapped in such a game is to accept, themselves, the very role scripted for them—to play consciously and better the game which they did not realize they had already been playing. Thus Isis, having discovered the real nature of the religion in which she has been brought up, decides to use it and to make it work more effectively, just as Kathryn Telman, in *The Business*, decides to fulfil what the Business wanted of her—marriage to the Prince of a Himalayan state—but for her *own* reasons rather than for theirs.

The games in which such characters are trapped are in turn versions of the structure of the universe itself, which is organized as a series of games at different levels, each level believing itself to be the ultimate truth until it is revealed to be no more than a piece in a game being played on another level. It is this structure that Banks self-consciously orchestrates in *Walking on Glass*. Graham Park believes himself to have fallen in love with Sara ffitch (sic), but to be threatened by a rival by the name of Stock. He has, however, been "stalked" by his friend Slater who is actually both Sara's brother and lover. Slater has played the role of Stock in order to conceal the reality of his incestuous relationship while Sara has encouraged Graham into being her lover as a decoy to prevent her real liaison being recognized. Graham's life, bounded by his feelings for Slater and for Sara, turns out to have been only a game, played out to help conceal the trangressive nature of their real relationship. At the same time, however, the denouement of the novel depends on the fact that another character, the mad Steven Grout, has put sugar in the petrol tank of Slater/Stock's motorbike. Slater's life is actually shaped by one of the mad games which Steven plays with reality since, for Steven, the world around him is only a fabrication designed to conceal the reality beyond it:

He took out the cassette recorder, switched the tape on. He had recorded the noise of the so-called "static" from the Short Wave band. But he knew what it really was: he listened to the grinding, deep, continuous roaring noise, and he recognised the sound of the War's eternal heavy bombers of the air. He was amazed that nobody else had noticed it. These were engines, that wasn't static. He *knew*. This was a Leak, a tiny slip they had made which let part of reality slip through into this prison of his life. (p. 113)

Park discovers his life to have been a game played by others; Steven believes his to be the only real life in a vast game that everyone else takes for reality.

Walking on Glass underwrites these layers of reality-turned-into-games, however, by having a third set of characters, Quiss and Ajayi, who are exiled in a ruined castle where they have to work out the rules of a series of games they are given to play. If they manage to play a game to a successful conclusion they are permitted to offer an answer to the riddle, "What happens when an unstoppable force meets an immovable object" (44). If the answer were to be correct then they could be realeased from exile back into their former lives. On one level, the relationship between the world that Quiss and Ajayi inhabit and the world of Park and Grout is analogic, since Quiss and Ajayi are like Slater and ffitch, condemned to endless games for their past crimes. On another level, Quiss and Ajayi may be simply characters in Steven Grout's fantasies, being versions of the old man and woman who also inhabit the hospital unit in which, at the novel's end, he is interminably confined:

An old man and an old woman sat in there, playing games over an old coffee table. Mr Williams took pieces from their games when they weren't looking, just for a laugh. He would give them the bits back later on, of course, so it wasn't really stealing, but, oh, it was funny watching them get all upset! (216)

It is Steven who broods over a matchbox which has on its packet the riddle which Quiss and Ajayi have to solve, their names signaled by the "Q" and "A" of the riddle's "question" and "answer". At the same time, because Quiss and Ajayi are presented as just as real in their particular chapters of the novel as any of the human characters in theirs, the novel implies that there is indeed another, more fundamental reality, a reality which contains the elemental war of which Grout dreams. Quiss and Ajayi are combatants "on their respective sides of the Wars", though the Wars are not the ultimate confrontation that Grout anticipates, since "they were not, of course, between Good and Evil at all, as non-combatants of every species always assumed, but between Banality and Interest" (p. 38).

The interaction of these various levels of reality in *Walking on Glass* becomes self-reflexive when, searching the castle to which they have been consigned, what Quiss discovers is that it contains a technology that allows him to be "inside somebody else's head" (p. 135), the head of someone on Earth thousands of years previously. The "real" world of human beings is a game being played by beings at a higher level of reality who use human consciousnesses to release them from the interminable boredom of their meaningless existences. The real world in which human beings think they decide and act is simply the vehicle through which those other beings act out games for their amusement—which is, of course, the "real" nature of characters in novels, whose supposedly "real" experiences are simply portions of a game played out to maintain our Interest and to avoid Banality. Novels presume to be a likeness of reality, but if reality is like a novel then we can never escape being pawns in others' games since we, as readers of novels, are those watchers of other characters who are trapped within the rules of a game they don't know they are playing: we are *complicit* in turning reality into a game.

SUBVERTING GENRES

Genre is one of the defining elements of the game of literature. The expectations of readers are shaped by their awareness that what they are reading belongs to a particular literary game, whether that game is gothic horror, romance, social realism or thriller (all of which have their role in *Complicity*). Iain Banks is a player of games with the rules of fiction, not just because, unusually, he writes both "serious" novels and science fiction novels, but because all of his novels, in either mode, are explorations of the possibilities of combining or disrupting the expectations of particular genres. Part of the bemusement that Banks's novels cause, even to his critical admirers, is that each novel plays a different game with the possibilities of genre, subverting the distinctions by which genres are defined and engaging in combinations — not to say copulations — of apparently incompatible genres.

In *The Wasp Factory*, Banks combined a first-person narrative of adolescent life with a Gothic novel of violence and horror. *The Wasp Factory* is shocking precisely because it turns the conventions of Gothic fiction, which readers are used to treating as belonging in a purely imaginary realm, into the assumed realities of ordinary life in the North of Scotland. In *Walking on Glass*, on the other hand, a conventional novel of contemporary manners and morals — the story of Park, Slater, and Sarah — is juxtaposed with a science fiction narrative in ways which question the validity of the genre of the novel of manners. If the universe is as the science fiction narrative tells us it is, and Slater and Sarah are no more than the vehicles of some other being's voyeurism, then the novel of manners has no validity, since it is founded on the notion of people's individual responsibility for their choices and for their actions. The boundaries which the traditional novel demands we respect if we are to treat it as "serious" fiction are precisely what Banks puts in question. In Banks's third "serious" novel, *The Bridge*, the relationship between what is presumed to be "reality" and what "fiction" is explored from the opposite perspective. In this case, the novel constructs an alternative world, the world of the Bridge, which we take to be real, but real only in the sense that fantasy asks us to suspend our disbelief and accept as real a world which does not correspond to the actualities of our own. This fantasy world, however, turns out to be the allegoric dreamworld of a man in a coma, a refracted version of the actualities of his life and of the world in which he has lived. We learn, in the course of the novel, to interpret the allegory and to see through it the real nature of a life which, told simply in itself, would have revealed almost nothing of the depths of the character's existence because they are depths of which he is not himself aware.

Such conflicts of style and genre in Banks's novels are designed to force us to recognize what any single genre would have to exclude, a dimension of reality that it could not adequately express. The effect of Banks's fiction is often like the scene from *Walking on Glass* when the "love story" that Parks thinks he has been living in is revealed to be a fiction, when he is translated from one genre of fiction into another:

It swelled in him then, like some wildfire cancer; a rapid disgust, a total allergy syndrome directed at everything around him; at the filthy, eviscerated mundanity of it all, the sheer crawling awfulness of existence; all the lies and the pain, the legalized murder, the privileged theft, the genocides and the hatreds and the stupefying human cruelties, all the starveling beauty of the burgeoning poor and the crippled in body and brain, all the life-defying squalor of the cities and the camps, all the sweltering frenetics of the creeds and the faiths, all the torturingly ingenious, carefully civilised savagery of the technology of pain and the economics of greed. (p. 238)

These are what the genre of his narrative—a love story of early manhood—exclude: the vast inhumanities of society and the insignificance of individual human beings are what can only be approached through an alternative genre that does not place the emotional life of one, well-off Western youth at its center. It is exactly that kind of cancer that afflicts Colley at the end of *Complicity*.

Given the games Banks plays with genre, it is no accident that critics tend to be most approving of *The Crow Road*, the novel which, as a young man's search for the clues to his family's past, has the most traditional structure, and to be least approving of novels such as *Canal Dreams*, which combine the elements of a realistic novel of social analysis with the form of the thriller. It is, however, the combination of the tradition of the serious novel with the elements of popular genre fiction—thriller, detective fiction, romance, fantasy or science fiction—that Banks requires if his novels are to confront the realities—and the brutalities—of modern existence and of the universe as revealed to us by modern science. What links *Canal Dreams* and *The Crow Road*, however, is Banks's use of a structure in which, as we move forward in the "present" time of the novel, we move back and forth across the protagonist's past to release the memory of those moments which have fundamentally shaped his or her existence. Banks's use of prolepsis and analepsis—flash forward, flash back—is crucial to his serious fiction, and none more so than *Complicity*. In each of them, however, the relationship between past and present also poses a question about what genre of narrative we are in. In *The Crow Road*, Prentice McHoan is caught up in a murder mystery, disentangling the disappearance of his Uncle Rory and the machinations of his Uncle Fergus; in *Complicity*, Cameron Colley is caught up in a political conspiracy involving multiple murders; in *Whit*, Isis is the inheritor of the religious schemes of her grandfather, which may simply be madness or may be a clue to the meaning of the universe. In each case, one kind of narrative—the narrative that explores the personal history of an individual's growth to maturity—is caught up in another kind of narrative, one which draws on the apparently simplifying forms of popular culture and genre fiction.

The combination of temporal disjunction with the subversion of genres leads Banks into complex uses of the role of his narrators. Frank in *The Wasp Factory*, for instance, narrates his own story in the first person as though unaware that that first person is really Frances. The knowledge which Frances already has, as the retrospective narrator, about her real identity is deliberately concealed from us, as readers, even although she reflects from her position of maturity on the significance of the events she describes. It is not that she is an unreliable narrator in the traditional sense—one from whose version of events we have to construct the true but concealed narrative; rather, she deliberately refuses to give us the key to her narrative until the point in the narrative at which she herself discovered that truth. A first-person, past tense narrative is, in effect, treated as though it were a present tense narrative. In *The Player of Games* a similarly ambiguous strategy is involved: at several points in the novel a strange quasi-authorial voice intrudes, questioning the construction of the narrative:

Does Gurgeh really understand what he's done, and what might happen to him? Has it even begun to occur to him that he might have been tricked? And does he really know what he's let himself in for?
    Of course not!
    That's part of the fun! (p. 100)

It is not until the last line of the novel we discover that this voice is actually the voice of the narrator and that the narrator is actually one of the characters in the novel — or, rather, two of the characters in the novel, since the first of them disappears out of the action at an early stage, and the fact that the second is the same person in disguise is not revealed till the last line. In other novels, Banks uses embedded first person narrators, as when, in *The Crow Road*, Rory's writings preserved on a primitive computer disk allow him to become, long after his death, a subsidiary first person narrator. In *A Song of Stone*, on the other hand, the first person narration appears to assure us that Abel will survive because, unless what we are reading is a written record, the first person narrator has to be still alive to tell it. However, *A Song of Stone* is narrated in the present tense: "Her head jerks up as I approach, and her hand comes up too, holding a pistol. I flinch, but the gun flies from her hand and clatters to the floorboards to one side" (p. 244). In this case, the use of the present tense allows a different play with the role of the

narrator, since the novel ends with Abel still alive, but awaiting the
death that will be his and the book's conclusion: "I face my future,
turn my back on a lifetime's desolation and on these dumb perse-
cutors . . . laugh at cheers that rise, buoying me, and with that salute
my end" (p. 280). We end on his end, as though the present in
which we read has become identical with the time in which the
events happen. Such interactions between the time of narration and
the time of experience, both the character's and the reader's, are
ones that Banks will exploit intensely in *Complicity*.

THE MATTER OF SCOTLAND

Banks had been writing for ten years before his fiction started to
appear in the mid-1980s, but publication of his work coincides with
a period of major transformation in Scottish writing, inspired by
political events of the 1970s and 1980s. The rise of Scottish Nationalism throughout the 1960s and 1970s had been reflected in an
increasingly self-confident Scottish literary culture, represented by
the work of poets such as Norman MacCaig and Edwin Morgan,
novelists like William McIlvanney and Allan Massie, and perhaps
most importantly, in terms of public impact, in the theatrical works
that John McGrath created for the 7:84 Theatre Company, such as
The Cheviot, The Stag and the Black, Black Oil (1973). The up-
surge of nationalism, both political and cultural, led to demands for
the re-establishment of the Scottish parliament, disbanded after the
Union with England in 1707, and in 1979 the Labour government
held a Referendum asking for support for a devolved Scottish parliament of very limited powers. The proposals were supported neither
by the Nationalists nor by the bulk of the Labour party's own
supporters in Scotland and produced only a tiny majority in favor
of a parliament — with over a third of people not voting. The Labour

government, already exhausted by industrial disputes and economic problems, refused to proceed. As a consequence, the Scottish Nationalists withdrew their support from Labour at Westminster and a General Election was forced at which the Conservatives, under Margaret Thatcher, were elected, inaugurating the decade that came to be identified with the radical free-market economics of Thatcherism.

In Scotland, bitter enmity between Labour and Nationalist supporters, both believing the other had made Thatcherism possible, increased as the consequences of Thatcherism — mass unemployment resulting from the decimation of traditional Scottish industries, the Falklands War, and the Poll Tax — became more evident. Many anticipated that Scotland, economically marginalized, politically divided, would become a cultural desert. In fact, however, the political energy that had been blocked by the Referendum went into cultural creativity, and the 1980s and 1990s saw an efflorescence of Scottish culture which many have described as a "renaissance". The publication of Alasdair Gray's *Lanark* in 1981 marked the turning point. Its combination of realism and fantasy, of historical recollection and invented futures opened the way for similar experiments in envisaging alternative Scotlands by many younger writers. In 1984 Gray's fellow Glaswegian James Kelman published *The Bus Conductor Hines*, a novel which adopted Scots vernacular speech as its primary medium and which made the use of Scots into a major area of experimentation in the following decade, culminating in the international success of Irvine Welsh's *Trainspotting*, written in Edinburgh working-class dialects, in 1993.

Having spent part of 1978 in the United States, Banks had gone to London in 1979 to try to find work, ending up as a costing clerk drawing up narratives for enormous legal bills. The briefest of authorial biographies in *The Bridge*, published in 1986, notes that "he lives in Kent", where he had moved to in 1984, but *The Bridge* itself testifies to the fact that he was profoundly conscious of developments in Scotland: as he has noted in interviews, *The Bridge's* combination of fantasy and realism was inspired by Gray's *Lanark*, which he described "as the best Scottish novel this century", while its use of Scots dialect shows the influence of Kelman's phonetic transcriptions of dialect speech. When *Espedair Street* was published in 1987, however, it was dedicated to "all [in] the People's Republic of Glenfinnan", a localized version of the as-yet-unrealized People's Republic of Scotland, and in 1988 Banks, like Dan Weir in that novel, became part of the returning diaspora of Scottish writers (such as the poet Douglas Dunn) who were committing themselves to the construction of a new Scotland, or to the rediscovery of an old one. Of the novels that followed, *The Crow Road*, *Complicity*, and *Whit* all foreground Scottish issues, and Banks's most recent novel, *The Business*, whose plot is global, still takes its starting point from the moment when the young Kathryn Telman is adopted from her home in a Scottish council house by a dynamic female executive. Banks has commented in interviews on the fact that he is often not counted as a Scottish writer, despite being a writer who was born in and lives in Scotland, but the matter of Scotland is clearly crucial to his work and there are at least four major themes of in Banks's fiction which derive from the Scottish tradition of the novel: (1) the double; (2) the fearful; (3) myth as an alternative to the history of modernity; (4) the primacy of the communal.

THE DOUBLE

The history of Scotland, divided between the Highlands and the Lowlands, between Scots and Gaelic or between Scots and English, between Protestant (John Knox) and Catholic (Mary Queen of Scots), has encouraged the idea of the Scots as a fundamentally

dualistic people, inheritors of a divided consciousness which expresses itself in terms of schizophrenia, doubles and repressed Others. Works such as James Hogg's *Confessions of a Justified Sinner*
(1824) or Robert Louis Stevenson's *Dr. Jekyll and Mr. Hyde* (1886)
have come to be taken as representative expressions of a theme
which is repeated in Gray's *Lanark*, whose central character lives
two lives, one as the failed artist Duncan Thaw in the Glasgow of
the 1950s and 1960s, and one as Lanark, a character trapped in a
fantasy world which, through the forms of fairy tale, repeats in
concealed form Thaw's life in the real Glasgow. Modern concern
with the double may derive not only from such traditions of Scottish
writing but from the work of the influential Scottish psychiatrist,
R. D. Laing, whose book *The Divided Self* (1957) analyzes schizophrenia in relation to a conception of the self as developed in the
work of the Scottish philosopher John Macmurray.

In Banks's novels Frank and Frances in *The Wasp Factory* represent a sexualized version of the double; in *The Bridge*, Orr knows
he has an alternative life somewhere else that he is trying to reconnect with; in *Espedair Street*, Daniel Weir is "weird" precisely because he has come to live a double life, being an internationally
famous rock star who poses as the caretaker of a converted Church
in Glasgow; while in *Canal Dreams* Hisako Onada is a Jekyll-and-
Hyde figure, both cellist and killer. In *The Crow Road*, Prentice
muses on the fact that,

> Sometimes I thought it was perfectly obvious that Fergus was utterly
> genuine, and all my ideas, all my suspicions were demonstrably ludicrous.
> Of course the man was innocent; I was insane. Guilty as charged, indeed;
> who was I to judge?
>   Other times it was as though his every inflection and gesture shrieked
> artifice, lies, deception. Very good deception, cunningly deployed lies and
> artful artifice, but everything false all the same. (p. 453)

The unresolved doubleness of Fergus's behavior is replicated in *Whit*, in which almost everyone is a double, acting out a concealed awareness of the distinctions between truth and fiction in their invented religion.

When Banks approaches the matter of Scotland, its history of double identities shapes the nature of his narratives and the presentation of his characters. They inhabit a world that is modern, rational, technological—like the world of Lowland Scotland as it was shaped by the Industrial Revolution—but they are conscious of another older, forgotten, world which, like the Highlands, sits alongside it. In *The Crow Road*, Prentice's father introduces him to a Scotland where you could touch "rocks two and a half billion years old; half as old as the Earth itself; a sixth of the age of the entire universe" (p. 308), a very different Scotland from the one that he discovers in urban Glasgow. Banks's Scottish characters, like Dan Weir in *Espedair Street*, escape to the Highlands to find their other selves, or travel to the Highlands, as Colley does in *Complicity*, to meet their dark double.

THE FEARFUL

Scottish Calvinism was built on the foundations of Old Testament religion, and the God of Calvin is a God of Vengeance as much as a God of Grace, inspiring terror rather than love. The most potent compliment in Scottish protestantism was that someone was "god fearing". As a consequence, notions of "fear" have played a crucial role in the Scottish intellectual tradition. J. G Frazer's *The Golden Bough* (1890), one of the seminal works of twentieth-century culture, was written in part to prove that human societies were founded not in love but in fear: human beings were, in their very formation, fearful. It is a truth which Salvador explores as he develops his alternative religion in *Whit*, a religion designed to transcend the fear of his Christian inheritance:

Salvador originally thought that there was a Devil—old Redtop as he sometimes referred to him—and that there was a Hell, too, a place submerged in eternal darkness whose walls were made of glass . . . Later, he was able to separate this fevered, fearful vision from the quiet calm articulation of perfection that is the true Voice of God, and realise that—again—what he had been experiencing was something from inside himself. These were his visions, not God's; they were the result of the fear and terror and guilty dread that exist in everyone and which certain faiths, especially Christianity, prey upon and exaggerate the better to control their flocks. (p. 226)

Salvador makes himself God-like by ceasing to be fearful, revealing the double sense of a word which can imply either one who *is* afraid or one who *inspires* fear in others. Man is fearful in the first sense because God is fearful in the second. In many Scottish novels, characters who aspire to escape their fears do so only by transforming themselves into something fear inspiring—effectively by taking upon themselves God's role in relation to the rest of humanity.

It is precisely this dialectic that shapes Frank's relationship to the world in *The Wasp Factory*. From being afraid s/he transforms him/herself into a fear inspiring creature; from being a (female) child at the mercy of the world, s/he makes him/herself the equal of the gods:

The Sea is a sort of mythological enemy and I make what you might call sacrifices to it in my soul, fearing it a little, respecting it as you're supposed to, but in many ways treating it as an equal. It does things to the world, and so do I; we should both be feared. (p. 43)

From making sacrifices out of fear, Frank asserts himself against the world until he too should be feared. Discovering the truth about her real identity reshapes Frank from being God-like in his thirst for revenge — "I murdered for revenge in each case, jealously exacting — through the only potency at my command — a toll from those who passed within my range" (p. 183) — to being, as Frances, an ordinary, a fearful human being: "I don't know what I'm going to do. I can't stay here, and I'm frightened of everywhere else" (p. 182).

The same dialectic drives many of Banks's characters and is divided between Andy and Colley in *Complicity*. Colley is like Dan Weir in *Espedair Street*, a "paranoid coward" (p. 37), and while Dan inspires physical fear in those around him — "I'm a monster, a mutant; a gangling ape; I scare children, I even scare some adults, come to that . . ." (p. 24) — Colley will end by releasing into the world a "monster" who has made a lot of people "terrified to open their doors" (p. 257). Andy is like Hisako in *Canal Dreams*, someone who emerges from being "so full of fearful hope and hopeless fear" (p. 114–15) to being a fear-inspiring and vengeful angel of death, immune to all fear because she is beyond life. The description of Hisako by the leader of the terrorists against whom she fights back — "dead and kicking" (p. 164) — might equally describe the terrorising "free radical" (p. 305) whom Colley helps to escape the law.

THE MYTHIC

One of the most significant books in twentieth-century Scottish literature is poet and critic Edwin Muir's *Autobiography*. In it he makes a distinction which is fundamental to his own poetry but which has also come to be seen as fundamental to the nature of modern Scottish literature, the distinction between the "story" and the "fable". For Muir, the "story" represents the ordinary events of everyday history; it is chronological and linear; each successive moment obliterates its predecessor, leaving nothing behind. The fable, on the other hand, represents the possibility of the eternal return of the same narrative structures, archetypal patterns which repeat themselves in the individual events of particular lives. The "story", for Muir, is the form of modern life, a life which lives simply from moment to moment towards the future; the "fable" is an alternative reality that we can only recover with difficulty from the depths of our memory but which redeems us from the endless and meaningless succession in which modernity entraps us.

The "story" and the "fable" represent one way of explaining what the social sciences of the late nineteenth and early twentieth centuries (in the work of Scottish thinkers like Robertson Smith and J. G. Frazer, as well as in the work of Freud and Jung whom they influenced) taught about the nature of human consciousness: that the human mind does not simply live in the knowledge provided by its own lifetime, but lives in and through structures which go back into the depths of prehistory, an archaeology of mind that goes back far beyond recorded history. Thus we live not only in the present but in the recovery, remaking, and reworking of ancient patterns that lie sedimented in our brains, patterns that return to us with the sense of ultimate truth precisely because they are so deeply ingrained in the depths of our consciousness. In modern Scottish fiction, the opposition of "fable" to "story" is also the opposition of "fable" to "history", since so much of the significance of modern experience is assumed to lie in its historical relevance, in the events which are "history making". It is the importance given to history that "fable" challenges: events have no significance unless they can be reincorporated into some mythic shape which reveals how they fit with the totality of human experience.

Because Scottish culture was so deeply engaged with the development of these ideas in the nineteenth century, they have proved remarkably productive for Scottish novelists in the twentieth century. Scottish writers, from Neil Gunn to Muriel Spark, have consistently focused on the possibility that narratives only make sense when we discover those mythic roots—of which Frazer's *The Golden Bough* is the storehouse—in which are revealed the true meanings of human experience. A major tradition of the Scottish novel, therefore, is built around the double narrative, in which the "story" of a particular life is shadowed, or doubled, by its mythic equivalent, and in which characters move between different dimensions of reality as they uncover the fable that gives meaning to their particular story. *The Bridge* is Banks's novel most clearly in this tradition, involving the suspension of the story of a modern life—suspended because of a car crash—and an entry into a mythic narrative where the real meanings of that life will be encountered through fables which involve cyclic repetitions rather than the constant progression of events in the "story".

The possibility of this alternative realm is what, in *The Crow Road*, Prentice McHoan is introduced to through one of his father's fables:

> "Well," he said, rolling slowly over and letting Lewis and Prentice slide off his back. He sat up; they sat down. "Way back, a long time ago, there were these big enormous animals that used to live in Scotland, and they—"
>
> "What did they look like, dad?" Prentice asked.
>
> "Ah." McHoan scratched his head through his brown curls. "Like . . . like big hairy elephants . . . with long necks. And these big animals—"
>
> "What were they called, please, Uncle Kenneth?"
>
> "They were called . . . mythosaurs, Helen, and they would swallow rocks . . . big rocks, way down into their crops, and they used these rocks to help crunch up their food. They were very very big animals, and very heavy because of all the rocks they carried around inside them. . . ." (30)

According to McHoan, the piles of rocks on the Scottish landscape are the leftovers from the death and decay of such mythosaurs, so that the rocks of Scotland are not simply geological formations, they are the material emblems of a past beyond the bounds of human experience. The mythic is, quite literally, scattered around the Scottish landscape, waiting to be recovered: "On walks, on day trips and holidays, he found and pointed out the signs that told of the past, deciphering the symbols written into the fabric of the land" (p. 307). That is why, late in the novel, the pregnancy of Verity (whose name gestures, of course, to "truth") is celebrated by a tour "around Gallanach [which] is thick with ancient monuments; burial sites, standing stones, henges and strangely carved rocks", a place "where you can hardly put your foot down without stepping on something that had religious significance to somebody sometime" (p. 397). The re-entry of the cyclic — fertilization and birth — into the sequential progress of history has to be experienced in terms of these remnants of the mythic, which gesture beyond ordinary time: "great flat faces of cup-and-ring marked rocks, their grainy surfaces covered in the concentric circular symbols that looked like ripples from something fallen in a pond, frozen in stone" (p. 397).

Edwin Muir believed that it was in dreams that we encountered this timeless realm of the mythic and dreams continually erupt into Banks's narratives not as elements of a character's consciousness but as though they were realities in themselves. In *Canal Dreams*, for instance, it is initially uncertain whether a passage such as the following is dream or reality:

Somebody had stabbed her. She had just woken up and she'd been stabbed; the knife hung from her belly, dripping blood. She tried to pull it out but couldn't. . . .She pulled the knife out and threw it into the lake. No blood rushed out of the wound, but the knife splashed when it hit, and some of the blood splattered her face and feet, and some hit the place where the knife had embedded, and single strand dribbled down to the lake at her feet, and the strand thickened, and pulsed, and the blood flowed into her not out of her, falling up out of the lake, as if a tap had been turned on. (pp. 145-7)

The passage begins as though it were simply the continuation of Hisako's horrific story but unfolds as a dream, a dream whose mythic elements will predict the future when she burns all of her enemies in a fire on the lake. In *A Song of Stone*, on the other hand, the whole novel seems to take place in the world of the "fable", a world to which the actualities of history are irrelevant and only the mythic patterns of things are significant. The "song of stone" is the Castle in which Abel has grown-up — both the genea- logical and the psychological fortress of the self, and like all the castles of Banks's fiction, representing an ancient home from which modern humanity is exiled.

We carry the silt of our own memories within us, like the castle's long- stored treasures, and we are top-heavy with it. But ours is geological in its profundity, reaching back through our shared histories, blood-lines and ancestries to the first farmers, the first hunting band, the first shared cave or nested tree. By our wit we look further back, and out, so that we bear the buried stripes of all our planet's earlier geology in the strata of our brains, and contain within our bodies the particular knowledge of the explosion of suns that lived and died before our own came into being. (pp. 196-7)

In *A Song of Stone* Abel lives through destruction of his castle, an allegory of the desolating destruction of humanity's loss of contact with the depths of its own being. The crises of Banks's novels turn on moments when the characters live not in the timescale of ordi- nary human experience — the timescale of "story" — but in the timescale of a universal "geology", a timescale of which only "fable" can make sense. The archetypal elements of life — earth, air, fire and water — provide much of symbolic development of Banks's writ-

ing and it is in those archetypal emblems of human community —
"Cities and Kingdoms and Bridges and Towers" (*The Bridge*,
p. 212) — that his characters have to find their true selves.

THE COMMUNAL

In the year of Iain Banks's birth, John Macmurray delivered the
Gifford Lectures at the University of Glasgow, later published as the
two volumes of *The Form of the Personal* (1957; 1961). He argued —
in a work increasingly recognized as among the earliest postmodernist challenges to the whole tradition of Western culture — that the
nature of human societies depended on the "communal mode", a
mode defined in terms of "heterocentricity", meaning "that the
centre of reference for the agent, when he seeks to act rightly, is
always the personal Other. To act rightly is then to act for the sake
of the Other and not for oneself" (*Persons in Relation*, p. 122). The
challenge in achieving a heterocentric morality is the "problem of
hostility resting upon fear, it demands the transformation of motives
by the overcoming of fear". Macmurray's writings gave philosophi-
cal expression to the communal ethos which had always underlain
Scottish traditions in religion and politics. After 1979, and the failure of the Devolution Referendum, the generally left-wing orienta-
tion of Scottish society was entirely at odds with the free-market
capitalism and rampant individualism promoted by successive
Thatcher governments. Defending Scottish communalism became
fundamental to the processes that were to lead, in 1997, to a second
Referendum which heralded the re-establishment of a Scottish parliament. Against that Thatcherite world of individual self-
aggrandisement — the world that Lennox in *The Bridge* has been
committed to before it leads him to the car crash that foretells the
"crash" of capitalism to come — Banks, like many other Scottish

writers of the 1980s, holds out the possibility of a communal existence in which people support rather than compete with one another.

The utopian social structure of "The Culture" in Banks's science
fiction novels is based precisely on this communal model, one
which regards individuality as achievable only in and through community rather than by defiance of it. As the drone Flere-Imsaho
explains to Gurgeh in *The Player of Games*, what is always in
opposition to culture are societies based not on communality but
on exploitation, because "it all boils down to ownership, possession;
about taking and *having*" (p. 210). Banks's protagonists are forced to
find a route back out of the world of "ownership", "of taking and
having" in order to rediscover the communities that they rejected
in their search for individual fulfillment. It is this sense of community from which rock stardom has alienated Daniel Weir in *Espedair Street*:

I watched the faces of the people in the bus, and I listened to their talk.
They seemed like real, proper, normal folk and I was the weird one all
right, I was the freak. Their lives, with all their diversities and complexities,
for all their sudden changes and surprising additions and omissions, must
have been of the ordinary stuff, the standard fare.

Mine seemed then to have been even more grotesque and deformed
than I'd feared in my darkest moments. The world belonged to these
people. I had had colossal effrontery contaminating it with my presence for
this long; now was time to pay, now it was time to admit life had been right
and I'd been wrong all the time, and dispose of this mutant frame, put to
rest this twisted, alien monstrosity. (p. 213)

The defense of the ordinary, the celebration of the ordinary is, for
Banks, crucial to the maintenance of civilized culture. The extraordinary narratives he weaves are based, in the end, on the possibility
of a return to a communality which has itself become extraordinary

because of the deformities of the modern world. As Kathryn Telman discovers, the reason the mythical Business that she works for survives is precisely because it understands how wrong is the Thatcherite emphasis on individualism: "We are individuals, but we need to co-operate" (p. 387).

2

The Novel

Like *Canal Dreams*, *Complicity* is novel which adopts the format of the thriller in order to explore the relationship between the present — a very recent present, since its main action takes place in 1992 and the novel was only published in 1993 — and the past; between a plot which is based on violent incidents in the present and their roots in the suppressed, forgotten violences of the past. In *Complicity*, however, the roots of the violence lie not in the destructive forces of the World War II but in the childhood experiences of the main characters. The repressed knowledge of concealed sexual violence in private life parallels the nature of an apparently peaceful society — post-World War II Britain — which is haunted by its violent history, a violent history which re-emerges in the form of the Falklands War of 1982. The Falklands War was represented at the time as the recollection and re-enactment of Britain's previous military achievements and its imperial role in the world. *Complicity* takes up the theme of violent re-enactment in every aspect of its characters' lives, from the personal and the sexual to the social and political. The modern world, that thinks it is liberal, liberated, libertarian, discovers that it is playing in a different narrative altogether: "This is a horror movie a fucking horror movie this lunatic is making his own horror film and you can't tell yourself Hell it's only a story aren't the special effects good it isn't real because that's exactly what it is" (p. 181). The horror that is played out in horror movies, contained safely—"it isn't real"—within the limits of genre fiction, is in fact the very image of modernity, unrecognized because "you can't tell yourself Hell", but Hell is where we are.

THATCHER'S AFTERMATH

The main action of *Complicity* is set in a very specific time frame, beginning with the anticipated publication of the report into the Orkney child abuse case of 1991 and ending shortly after Bill Clinton has defeated George Bush in the American Presidential elections in November 1992. It takes place, therefore, in the aftermath of Thatcherism, in the period when her "grey ghost", John Major, had taken over as Prime Minister and maintained her legacy by winning the election of April 1992. It also takes place in the aftermath of the collapse of communism in 1989 and the first war of the "New World Order" in the "Desert Storm" campaign against Iraq. It was a time defined by Francis Fukuyama's influential article, "The End of History", which argued that there was now no alternative to the economics of capitalism and to the ideology of liberal individualism, so that the conflicts between ideologies which had been the burden of modern history had finally come to an end.

The main portion of the first chapter of *Complicity*, entitled "Independent Deterrent" invokes the West's unconstrained military domination in the passage of a nuclear submarine into its Scottish base at the Gare Loch. The vast power of modern weaponry is dramatized by the ineffectual efforts of the protesters from the Campaign for Nuclear Disarmament to stop its progress. As the protagonist of the novel, Cameron Colley, a journalist with the *Caledonian* newspaper in Edinburgh (a thinly disguised version of the *Scotsman*) comments, the destructive power of the submarine's nuclear weaponry has, after the fall of communism, become an irrelevance ("what was always obscene — and definitively, deliberately useless — becomes pointless") — but its real point was precisely that the cost of such weaponry, and the attempt to match it, is what "broke the communist bank, finally devastating a Soviet system no longer able to compete" (p. 15). The submarine, part of Britain's policy of "independent deterrence", ensures that Britain retains its role and status as one of the leading nations of the world, despite the fact that its economy and its military might are actually "dependent" on those of the United States. Britain is a "dependent" rather than an "independent" power, one built more on fantasy than reality.

From his student days, Colley has remained a left-wing socialist in his political views, defying his friends Andy and William, both of whom had become convinced of Thatcherism's effectiveness.

"They lied to get in," I say. "They'll lie to try and stay in. How can you trust them?"

"I trust them to try and sort out the unions," William says.

"It was time for a change," Andy says.

"Country needs a kick up the fucking bum," William agrees, defiantly.

I'm horrified. "I am surrounded by selfish bastards I thought were my friends," I say slapping my forehead with the hand holding the J and almost setting my hair alight. (p. 187)

The careers of William and Andy are constructed to be representative of the Thatcherite era. William goes from being a Business Studies student to working for an American computer firm based in Scotland's "Silicon Glen" (p. 64), one of the new high-tech companies that have replaced the traditional heavy industries decimated in the early years of the Thatcher decade. William's wife, Yvonne is also in a new growth industry of the Thatcher era—bankruptcy management, a specialist in "easing the death throes of failing businesses" (p. 65). Andy, on the other hand, is a veteran of the Falklands War, that symbolic re-enactment of Britain's World War II glories. Having returned to civilian life he works in the glamorous industry of the period, advertising, and then becomes that other icon of Thatcherite Britain, a retail entrepreneur, opening a business called *The Gadget Shop*, which is based on the marketing of expensive executive toys.

Margaret Thatcher once famously asserted that there was no such thing as society; the sense of lost community afflicts Colley when he recollects his student days because all four of them have become, in various ways, "selfish bastards". Colley and Yvonne, for instance, are lovers who delight in taking chances by secret sexual interaction with one another while William is present: "She's playing footsie with me under the table, her shoe off, her black nylon foot stroking my right calf" (p. 64). Their relationship, however, is based entirely on her use of him as a sexual substitute for William's unimaginative lovemaking:

"Cameron, I've no intention of leaving William."

I shrugged again, sorry I'd asked now. "Like I say, it just occurred to me."

"Well un-occur it." She glanced at where William was bumping enthusiastically across the waves, miraculously still upright. She put out a hand and briefly touched my arm. "Cameron", she said, and her voice was tender, "you're the excitement in my life; you do things for me William couldn't even imagine. But he's my husband, and even if we do go astray now and again, we'll always be an item." (p. 217)

The business nature of their relationship is underscored when Yvonne comments, about Colley's having tried to get another woman into bed, "I'd have given you a reference, Cameron" (p. 207).

Colley, however, does not represent any real opposition to his Thatcherite environment. In a world in which "there is no alternative", as Thatcher declared, his socialist commitments are as shallow as his personal relationships. Despite the fact that he proposes, in a party conversation, that he would turn all middle-class people into "bone meal" after the revolution (p. 206), he is passionately committed to consuming the products of international globalized capitalism — like the new Toshiba computer he buys, like the Peugeot car he drives, and, especially, like the drugs he consumes. Socialism is a cynical stance that allows him to stand outside of the values of his friends but makes no real demands on the way he lives. His role as a journalist gives him the opportunity to write critically about his society but the driving force of his writing is not social responsibility but personal gratification: achieving a front-page story gives him "a modest thrill of news-fix; a doze of journo-buzz. This is a kind of hit unique to the profession: near-instant in-print gratification" (p. 24). For Colley, journalism is not a vocation but an addiction, another of the "fixes" that allow him continually to enhance his psychic reality at the expense of personal or social responsibility. He may try to write a piece to reveal the corruption of the whisky industry in Scotland because it has adulterated its products to suit the American market, but he drives to the distillery to get his information in complete denial of any communal responsibility: "once up to cruising speed — needle in that 85-to-90 region the jam-sandwich boys ignore unless they're particularly bored or in a *really* bad mood — steer with knees while rolling spliff, feeling good in a childish way and laughing at myself and thinking, *Don't try doing this at home, kids*" (p. 29).

Colley's "childish" retreat from adult responsibility is at one with the "infantile" culture that produces the "expensive executive toys" (pp. 203–4) from which Andy makes his money and the Thatcherism that Andy describes as "the children's crusade to recover the lost citadel of British economic power" (p. 141). Colley, despite his political views, has become more and more engrossed by the very values of the Thatcherism he rejects. His constant use of tradenames and nicknames for all the gadgets he uses — "Take the bleeper, mobile, Tosh, NiCads and slot-in radio down to the 205" (p. 29) — reveals someone entirely consumed by the consumer society of which he is a part, someone who is more concerned with getting additional credit on his credit card than taking credit from his political stance. Colley can only cope with this evasion of his underlying values by maintaining his distance from reality through a constant balancing of various chemicals, legal and illegal, adulterated and pure — "A double whisky doesn't take too long to knock back, and keeps the system in equilibrium, what with the speed aboard" (p. 20). When Colley is forced to acknowledge in the later stages of the narrative is that "I'm just like everybody else: selfish" (p. 235) he is not announcing a truth of human nature — only his own complete absorption into the ethos of Thatcherism.

Throughout the novel, Andy is Colley's mirror-image, his twin in whom the same themes develop in the opposite direction. Thus while Colley becomes more implicitly Thatcherite in his behavior, Andy's outright commitment to Thatcherism in their student days has turned to disillusionment:

"Well, here we are," Andy says, sitting forward and slapping his hands on his knees, then taking the J when I tap him on the elbow. "Thanks." He tokes on the spliff. "Here we are and we've had our experiment; there's been one party, one dominant idea, one fully followed plan, one strong leader — and her grey shadow — and it's all turned to shit and ashes. Industrial base cut so close to the bone the marrow's leaking out, the old vaguely socialist inefficiencies replaced with more rabid capitalist ones, power centralised, corruption institutionalised, and a generation created which'll never have any skills beyond opening a car with a coat hanger and knowing which solvents give you the best buzz with a plastic bag over your head before you throw up or pass out." (p. 141)

While Colley is sucked into the Thatcherite world, but retreats from it through drugs, Andy retreats physically from it, withdrawing from his business into living in a broken-down Highland hotel where he nurses his grievances against a system which has failed to deliver the transformation of society that he had hoped for. But while Colley has excused himself from all responsibilities, Andy has come to the opposite conclusion: "We all have the responsibility, Cameron. You can't escape it" (p. 142), a responsibility he will carry out by becoming a personal version of the "independent deterrent" which Thatcherite politics extolled. Colley may cynically look on his fellow journalists as his "accomplice hacks" (p. 17), but Andy points to the much deeper *complicity* they both share with the values of a world they scorn.

PLAYING GAMES

Colley's childishness and complicity are symbolized by the computer games with which he is obsessed, games which mimic a world of economic and military power that is the real world of the 1990s but which pretend that that world is open to the control of a single individual:

The little hand sprite on the screen flashes from control surface to display, grabbing icons and throwing them about my empire like thunderbolts, building roads, dredging ports, burning forests, digging mines and — using the very ironic Icon icon — opening more temples to myself (p. 55)

The vast forces that overwhelm the "self" in the real world are, within the workings of this game, made subservient to the autonomous "self" of the modern man. Colley becomes dominator of society, his strategies mirroring those that he objects to in the real world around him while revealing how much he is shaped by them:

I have a brainwave and get my secret police to go down to the bazaar and find some drug dealers; bingo! The dealers are introduced to the Court and soon most of the people I've been working on are thoroughly hooked. It occurs to me this might actually be a better way of controlling things than just bumping people off, which is what the secret police are usually best at. (p. 55)

The computer game inducts Colley into appreciative exploitation of the very values he claims to resist in the real world, taking "great delight in ordering the ceremonial execution of several generals" (p. 78). Playing such games, full of violence and destruction, is, for him, "just possibly better than sex" (p. 54), but they are simply a mirror-image of the sexual games he plays with Yvonne which are based, equally, not on love and commitment but on violence and coercion: "I'm kneeling on the bed, stretched backwards with my legs apart and my wrists tied to my ankles with silk scarves" (p. 93). Indeed, one of the games is for Colley to simulate breaking and entering into Yvonne's house and raping her at knifepoint: "I force her back down into the bed, hand still over her mouth. I raise the knife so she can see it . . . I rest the blade of the knife against her throat and she goes still" (p. 128). The violence from which Yvonne's sexual pleasure derives is the analogue of the war games her husband plays, during one of which he catches Colley with his gun jammed: as "he just walked forward slowly shooting me" Colley wonders "does he know about me and Yvonne? Has he guessed, has somebody told him, is this what all this is about?" (p. 219). Game and reality merge into one another. Playing with violence and enacting real violence become indistinguishable from one another. So that the language that Colley uses casually when Yvonne and William have a argument with another car owner—" 'Shoot the lot of them,' I said, thinking about getting out and having a cigarette"—turns threateningly real in William's response: "People might be a bit more polite if everybody carried guns" (p. 218).

In *Complicity*, reality and games are accomplices of one another. Playing games is not an alternative to a violent reality but a preparation for accepting that reality. It is precisely by playing a violent game with reality that Colley becomes a murder suspect. In a television review in his newspaper, Colley has suggested that

> . . . somebody should make one of these programmes for those of us who're fed up seeing the usual suspects get theirs (corrupt landlords, substance-abusing youths and of course the inevitable drug dealers; reprehensible villains all, no doubt, but too predictable, too *safe*) and introduce a Real Avenger, a Radical Equaliser who'll take on some alternative hate-figures. Somebody who'll give people like James Anderton, Judge Jamieson and Sir Toby Bissett a taste of their own medicine . . . (p. 108)

Colley's play with reality, his invention of an alternative kind of television program, becomes the source of the series of murders of which he is accused. The people Colley names are assaulted and murdered by someone not simply *imagining* the possibility of a Radical Equaliser, but acting it out for real. When questioned by the police, Colley has no alibi for the latest of the killings because he was at home all night "playing computer games" (p. 109). The adult who has treated life as a game is reduced to declaring, "I feel like I'm a child again, like I'm up before the headmaster" (p. 109), as though it is a relevant moral response to retreat into the world of childhood where games remain separate from reality.

Colley's sense of his own significance as a reporter on the track of a government conspiracy to cover up the deaths of several men involved in secret research work is equally self-deceiving, since it too is based on repeating the past. It is a repetition of the most famous instance of investigative journalism in the modern era, Woodward and Bernstein's discovery of U.S. President Richard Nixon's complicity in a dirty tricks campaign against his political opponents in 1974, the so-called "Watergate Affair". Woodward and Bernstein had a mole inside the government, known as "Deep Throat", who fed them information and guided their investigations. Colley has a similar mole, Mr. Archer, who is providing him with hints about how to investigate the deaths. Colley, however, is the one who is actually the subject of the conspiracy and the dirty tricks, since Archer is Andy, arranging that Colley will always be somewhere on his own when the real murders—those Andy is carrying out—are happening. Colley thinks he knows the rules of the game he is playing—those defined by "Watergate"—but he is caught in a game in which he is a piece on the board rather than the player making the moves.

Colley's ignorance of the relationship between reality and game in the present is the distorted reflection of the fact that he has suppressed all knowledge of crucial moments in his past when games were transformed into deadly realities. Confronted with the possibility of his responsibility for the crimes of the Radical Equaliser, the adult Colley can declare, "I hate the Tories and all their accomplices, but I'm not a fucking *murderer*, for Christ's sake" (p. 110)—except that he knows that this is a lie, that as a child he actually *was* a murderer. Underlying his friendship with Andy is a dark truth which neither of them have ever acknowledged, the time when a childhood game with their developing sexuality—Andy encourages Colley to jerk him off because although "it's not the same as being with a girl . . . people do it" (p. 197)—is intruded upon by an adult, claiming to be a policeman, who turns their playful sexual exploration into a real sexual assault:

> "You've no right being here," Andy says, sounding frightened. "This is private property."
> "Oh is it?" the man says. "Private property, is it? And that give you the right to do dirty, perverted things, does it?" (p. 232)

The boundaries of the private game with the possibilities of their maturing sexuality are broken, turning them into accomplices in a public act that is beyond the law. Having put themselves beyond the boundaries of adult law they become victims of an all too real piece of adult "play" when the "policeman" attempts to have sex with Andy. Colley comes to Andy's rescue by battering the man over the head with a branch, after which Andy takes the branch and "brings it crashing down on the back of the man's head; once, twice, three times" (p. 239). The accomplices in an "innocent" game have become accomplices in a real crime. They have transgressed across the boundary that divides games from reality, that reveals the extent to which reality is nothing but a series of games.

NARRATIVE DOUBLES

Complicity, like all of Banks's novels, also plays games with genre. In this case Banks has constructed a crime thriller around that iconic figure of the late twentieth century, the serial murderer, most famously represented in popular culture in the character of Hannibal Lector in *Silence of the Lambs*, but recalled in the novel itself by the case of Dennis Nilsen, the British serial killer, whom the detective interviewing Colley is also supposed to have interviewed (p. 114). The serial murderer is terrifying because his murders are not crimes of passion but part of a calculated assault upon the values of society, a deliberate rejection of the boundaries of any common morality. The novel develops, however, into one of the classic forms of the traditional "serious" novel—the personal narrative of the recollection of the lost self of childhood or adolescence. In modern Scottish literature this is most famously represented by Neil Gunn's *Highland River* (1937), but it is also the form of novels such as Kurt Vonnegut's *Slaughterhouse Five* (1968), which probably influenced the combination of realism and science fiction in Banks's *Walking on Glass*. In both these novels, events are represented in disjunctive timeframes: as we move forward in narrative time in the "contemporary" world of the novel, so we move backwards in personal time to uncover the forgotten experiences of an earlier stage of life. The fact that in *Complicity* the forgotten childhood experiences turn out to be potentially criminal acts makes Colley into the investigator not of a government conspiracy to repress the truth of its double-dealing, but of his private conspiracy to repress his recollection of personal guilt. Like Oedipus in Sophocles' play, *Oedipus Rex*, Colley is the guilty origin of the very contagion whose source he is trying to discover.

The double movement of this narrative structure is compounded by the use of a double narrative voice, with first person narration of the major portion of the novel— "I put the glasses down and let them hang from my neck while I light another Silk Cut" (p. 10)—interleaved with sections, principally but not exclusively the sections dealing with the murders, that are narrated by a self-addressing "you":

Then the door closes and they are there in front of you and in that instant you see him turned slightly away, putting his briefcase down on the table beside the answer-machine. The girl—blonde, tan, mid-twenties, holding a slim briefcase—glances at you. She does a double-take. You are smiling behind the mask, putting one finger up to your lips. (6)

This narrative technique is a famous one in Scottish writing, used extensively by Lewis Grassic Gibbon in *Sunset Song* (1932), often cited as the greatest of twentieth-century Scottish novels, but also used more recently by James Kelman, whose first-person narrators regularly address themselves as "you". The implication of such a strategy, in Gibbon as it is in Kelman, is of the divided nature of the self which addresses itself as though it was another, a "you" rather than an "I". In *Complicity*, the reader is kept in ignorance of who the "you" is, while the simple juxtaposition of the narrative events suggests that it might be Colley. His name, both parts of which could be surnames, might be the indicator of the fact that he operates on two levels, Cameron and Colley, the "you" and the "I", two identities which have no knowledge of each other; our ignorance of who "you" is might be shared by Colley even while he is himself the perpetrator of events of which he retains no conscious memory. Thus the first six pages of the novel are narrated by the "you" voice, describing the murder of Sir Toby but then switches to an apparent third person — "It's a clear cold October day" — which transfers into the first person: "Further round still, towards the head of the loch, I can make out gantries . . ." (p. 9): the continuity of the narrative is designed to suggest that we are dealing with a single character represented by different grammatical forms. The narrative technique, of course, tells a truth which the novel will unfold: that Cameron and Andy are indeed two sides of the same personality, an "I" and a "you" whose mutual dependency goes much deeper than Colley realizes when he thinks of Andy as his "old soul-mate, my surrogate brother, my other me" (p. 29). The "you" voice of the murderer will be revealed not to be Colley's but Colley will be revealed to be nonetheless *complicit* with its actions. The *complicity*, however, also points out towards the reader, the "you" whom the narrative also addresses: we are all equally guilty of the consequences of our society's actions.

Maintaining the possibility of Colley's double identity, as both "I" and "you", is crucial to our first reading of *Complicity*, though on a second reading we become aware of the subtleties that Banks has built into these narrative games. When the girl in the above passage does "a double-take" the word "double" points to the possibility of a "doppelganger", a malignant second self, and when Colley calls Andy on the phone he inquires, "Andy, is that you?" (p. 73), pointing us secretly towards the question we should be asking: "You, is that Andy?" By having one section — the opening of Chapter 6, "Exocet Deck" — in which Colley himself "plays" the role of housebreaker and attacker in his pretended assault upon Yvonne, Banks keeps alive the possibility that the "I" and the "you" are the same person — until the moment when Colley, in Chapter 8, is confronted with the fact that the killer is probably someone he knows, even although at this point the possible identity of the murderer is concealed by the fact that Andy is presumed to be dead. In the novel's final section, however, Banks switches back to presenting Colley's final scene through the "you" voice: "You light a cigarette, shake your head as you look out over the grey enthroned city, and laugh" (p. 313). Colley as the object of the self-addressing "you" emphasizes not only the extent to which he has become detached from his own identity but the extent to which, without having himself committed the murders, he is now identified with the voice of the murderer whom he has helped to escape.

The narrative of the violent "second self" whose real identity has to be kept secret from the reader by a double (or, indeed, treble) narrative voices is a traditional one in Scottish fiction. It stems from James Hogg's *Confessions of a Justified Sinner* (1824), in which Robert Wringhim discovers that he — or, as he claims, someone impersonating himself — has been committing a horrific series of murders. Robert Louis Stevenson's *Dr. Jekyll and Mr Hyde* (1886) has Jekyll transform himself chemically into Hyde in order to carry out less specified but no less horrific acts of violence. What is significant about both narratives is that they develop from a retrospective narrative into a narrative that concludes in the present tense, with the protagonist writing down his experiences as they happen. Such narratives have a disturbing immediacy that derives from their withdrawal of the distance that traditional, past-tense, third-person narrative provides, a distance that assures us the narrative action is already completed before we started to read it.

Banks had explored the interaction of past-tense and present-tense narratives in *The Bridge*, where Orr's "dreams" happen in the past tense, and his "life" — which is actually Lennox's "dream" in his coma — happens in the present tense. Lennox's real past, on the other hand, is narrated in the past tense, as though it was indistinguishable from his dreams. In *Complicity*, the present tense is used both for the events which are part of contemporary narrative time — 1992, the year of the parliamentary debate of the Maastricht Treaty and Bill Clinton's electoral victory — and, equally, for events which belong to the past. Events from Colley's childhood, his years at the university or his early days as a journalist, all appear in the novel in the present tense, disrupting our sense of the relationship between earlier and later events. By resisting any sense of temporal priority, the mode of the narration resists — like Colley himself — the possibility of establishing causal connections by which the events can be explained. Two present tenses — the present tense of childhood and the present tense of the murders in 1992 — cannot be related (causally) to each other precisely because the style in which they are related makes them into autonomous moments, existing only in and having effects only on an immediate present.

The constant to-and-fro of the novel's shifting time-sequences emphasizes the disruption of the relationship between past and present that makes Colley amnesiac about his past and makes Andy continually mindful of it. The terror of recollection is so intense precisely because the moment of the murder of the boys' attacker is also a moment that forces Colley to relive — as though it were present again — his earlier traumatic experience when Andy, aged seven, falls through the ice on a frozen river and Colley deserts him. As he runs away he can hear Andy call "get a branch" and it is the memory of that call that brings him back, nearly ten years later, with the branch they use to commit the murder. Andy's call has, as it were, become disconnected from the normal sequence of cause and effect: it has no effect in the first incident but is effective ten years later in the second. This breakdown of the causal sequence of events is enacted in many aspects of the narrative: we are given, for instance, references to Andy as "the ice-child" (p. 76), "the ice boy" (p. 138) before we know anything about the incident which justifies the adjective. It is an unmotivated expression which will only be explicable when time is run backwards to reconnect Colley's traumatic history, which is why the dream sequence on page 147 appears, on first reading, to dramatise a sudden acceleration of time, turning the summer scene of two boys naked on the grass into a winter scene in which the "trees are bare and black". In fact, however, the two scenes exist in a reversal of time, the summer scene being later and being connected to the earlier one through Colley's repeated betrayal of Andy: Colley is himself accelerating towards the future only to confront the past.

There is, however, a particular moment when the present-tense narrative reveals itself to be a game, a game which *allows* Colley to deceive both us and himself:

I lied about something. Earlier. I told it the way it felt, not as it actually was. Or the way it feels and actually is. Whatever. (p. 183)

By acknowledging that he is "telling" and that there is a narrative time to the telling as well as to the events being told, Colley reveals that the present-tense narrative is actually a *retelling* whose apparent immediacy has a double purpose: it is both an attempt to preserve the purity of the past by not allowing it to be seen through the experience of adulthood, and a denial that childhood events can still be present in the shaping of adult consciousness. This structure is made explicit in Chapter 9 when Colley is invited by McDunn, the police officer who believes he is not the killer, to "Just think" about who among his acquaintances the killer might be. Colley's recollections of his past—punctuated by "I'm thinking" (p. 202), "Still thinking" (p. 208, p. 215)—occur initially in the immediate present tense that is typical of the narrative as a whole, but it then switches to the past tense as Colley begins to see the connections between past and present. These recollections immediately precede the present tense relation of the murder of the boys' attacker in Chapter 10: Colley's suppression of all memory of the murder has turned his unacknowledged past into a continuing presence, an permanent possibility haunting his life, always waiting to replay itself in the present. When Andy phones to alert the police to his murder of William, he announces it as being "a present" (p. 269) left for Colley: each death is an exorcism of a past that remains always present between them, which is why the conspiracy which Andy invents for Colley to investigate is called "Ares"—not only the god of massacre but also of events that never become past, that always "are".

There is one further repressed moment which Colley's narrative conceals from us until almost the end of the narrative. It is the much more recent moment of his journey as a war correspondent to the scene of the Allied bombing of Iraqi forces on the Basra Road, only to discover that he has nothing to say about the horrors of war, that they are too horrific to be recounted. Again the relation of experience to its understanding fails: "I was reduced to a numb, dumb realisation of our unboundedly resourceful talent for bloody hatred and mad waste, but stripped of the means to describe and present that knowledge" (p. 290). Colley's suppressed experience parallels Andy's in the Falklands. Andy feels again that he has been betrayed, this time by the incompetence his commanding officer. Colley's betrayal is of his moral responsibility to tell the truth. What had been their private experiences of betrayal and repression become personal versions of the large-scale betrayal and suppression that is Western culture, a culture whose public narrative is of ever-increasing freedom and liberty and material progress but which is constantly shadowed by its dark other, the forgotten history of world-wide violence and repression on which its security is based.

FEARFUL SELVES

When Colley goes to the Highlands to visit Andy he plays a computer game called *Xerium* (one of Banks's many invented games) and is shown finally how to cross beyond a limit which has always defeated him. Andy tells him, "You're not gung-ho enough" and Andy's friend Howie adds, "Aye; you've got to be a real man to play this game" (p. 136). The following night, "A gust of wind throws rain against the window and shakes the frame; it's loud and surprising and I flinch but he just turns round slowly and looks out into the darkness with what could almost be contempt" (p. 146). Andy is the fearless self to Colley's timid one. Colley plays at bravery — "you ferry a dump of fuel, shielding, a nuke and a missile, load up on fuel and a nuke, fly out and up eight clicks" (p. 135) — just as he *plays* at breaking and entering and rape; while Andy, Falklands veteran who understands real missiles — his only nightmare is "about being blown to fuck by a missile, ten years ago" (p. 145) — is prepared to carry out the assaults for real. The defining moment of their childhood is one which exemplifies their roles as the fearful and the fearless. Ordered not to go on to the ice on the river "Andy just whooped and jumped down onto the boulder-lumped white slope of shore and sprinted out across the pure flat snow towards the far bank", while Colley looks on, "frightened for him" but with a sudden "rush of joy" at his daring. When Andy falls through the ice, the language describing Colley's feelings becomes a thesaurus of fear: "I'm yelling in fear now", "I'm screaming so hard, wetting my pants as I squeeze the screams out", "I'm stuck there terrified", "I'm petrified" (p. 159). The moment of fearful petrification repeats itself when they are attacked in the woods: "I lie there, gulping for air, terrified of the man coming to get me while I lie there helpless" (p. 238). From that moment, fear becomes the underlying reality of Colley's life, a fear which he covers with the cynical, hard-boiled, shallow assertiveness of the journalist, and tries to escape through his various addictions.

The consequences of Colley's evasion of the past is dramatized when Colley, drunk in the Cafe Royal, believes that he has disappeared, that he has been reduced to an absence: *"things are not right*; I can see those bottles on the gallery ahead of me, and I can see their reflections behind them, but *I can't see me! I can't see my own reflection"* (p. 114). The mirror in which he is searching for himself is in fact only an empty space but the empty space is his real reflection, the reflected emptiness of his assumed personality. Andy, on the other hand, also disappears, but disappears by killing his acquaintance Howie and burning the body so that it will be taken to be his own. In Howie's death we witness the repetition of the boys' killing, and are given an image of how that killing was also the killing of them: "You bring the log down with all your might. It hits his head and you don't hear the noise it makes because you cry out at the same time, as though it's you in the bed, you being attacked, you being killed" (p. 177). Colley disappears in terror—even in his dreams he "knows how to turn away from this

"Y", which not only negates her feminine name but suggests masculinity by the fact that the Y-chromosome is the male chromosome. Equally, she refers to him as "bitch-boy" (p. 132) and is unsatisfied by his sexual assault on her until he mounts her from the rear, as though in a homosexual coupling. A sexual preference for the masculine is also implied in William's greeting to Andy when he is first introduced, "So you're Cam's soldier boy" (p. 184). Colley's own behaviour points sometimes towards a repressed homoeroticism. Drunk after an evening with his friend Al he believes that flowers Al has bought are for him, and is confused when he is told they are for Andi, mistaking Al's wife's name for Andy's and making us aware of the Y that connects Yvonne to Andy. Drunk at Andy's hotel, Colley relates that

I put an arm round Andy's neck at one point and say, You know I love you, old buddy, and isn't friendship and love what's it's really all about? and why can't people just see that and just be *nice* to each other? except that there just so *many* complete bastards in the world, but Andy shakes his head and I try to kiss him. . . . (p. 146)

The "love" for Andy which can only express itself when Colley is drunk points back to fact that their childhood homoeroticism was pre-empted by the grotesque interruption of an adult sexuality, and points back to their homosexuality as suspended and unfulfilled rather than forgotten.

Colley believes that his betrayals of Andy are the two childhood moments when he ran away, but there is another crucial moment in their relationship, the moment when, as students, Yvonne leaves William's bed and comes to Colley's and makes love to him. Not realizing that Andy is also in the same room, in his sleeping bag, Yvonne tells Colley "This never happened". After she leaves,

I lift my head up and look down to the floor at the foot of the bed, where Andy is lying curled up in his sleeping bag, unseen in the shadows, which is why *I* was being quiet.

"Andy?" I whisper quietly, thinking that maybe he slept through it all.

"Lucky fucking bastard," he says in a normal voice.

I lie back, laughing silently. (p. 189)

The immediate meaning of the passage points to Andy's envy of Colley's "fucking", making him the "lucky . . . bastard". However, the word "lie" in this passage connects directly to Colley's narratorial lie, "I lied about something" (p. 183), which introduced this section of the novel, and what he has lied about is the fact that Andy does not know about his relationship with Yvonne: "I don't want Andy to know about me and Yvonne", he tells us, *as though* Andy has no knowledge of their relationship at all: "This is awkward because Andy knows Yvonne and William from our Stirling days; he used to be really friendly with William and, though they seem to have gone their separate ways, I don't want Andy to know about me and Yvonne" (p. 74). What the later acknowledgment of the "lie" reveals is that Andy has every reason to suspect that Colley's married lover is Yvonne: "Frightened I'll tell somebody?" Andy asks, and Colley replies, "Yeah. I live in perpetual fear our enormous circle of mutual friends will find out" (p. 75). Colley's irony reveals the truth: their very small circle of mutual friends could easily betray him, since Andy has possible reason to want retribution for Colley's betrayals of him.

The significance of Colley's narratorial lie to the readers and of his personal evasion with Andy is pointed up when Andy leaves the fingers of one of his final victims laid out in the window of a fishshop: "Andy had used the doc's fingers to spell out I LIED on the counter" (p. 268). To the police, this reads as Andy's acknowledgment of the fact that he had promised not to kill the doctor;

place ... how to escape from it" (p. 22)—while Andy turns his original act of vengeance—the killing of the policeman—into the fundamental ethic of his life, a determination to take revenge upon the world and to terrorize it. Trying to live entirely in the present, Colley is forced back insistently into the past, while Andy, always mindful of the betrayals of the past, tries to anticipate the future by bringing forward the Day of Judgment, ensuring immediate retribution for all the crimes he sees the world to be afflicted by.

Colley continually escapes from his fears through addictions of various kinds but by doing so he is, effectively, creating a substitute religion. When, as a child, he takes his first cigarette, he discovers that he has been "joined mystically with the universe", that he has had "a revelation, an epiphany": "This was better than religion, or this was what people always *meant* by religion! The whole point was that *this* worked ... nothing fucking well *delivered* like they did. They were truth. Everything else was falsehood" (p. 47). It is a religion which redeems him by abolishing fear. Andy, however, is a redeemer of another kind who exists to recreate a world of terror: Colley's "double", "his other self", has developed from being merely fearless—"Never fear, sis" he says to Clare (p. 46)—to being fear-inspiring, someone who exists only to force others to confront their hidden fears, "this prophet of reprisal, this jealous, vengeful, unforgiving son of our bastard commonwealth of greed" (p. 289). Andy is the son of God who does not invert his Father's vengeful sternness, replacing punishment with forgiveness but carries through a relentless religion of vengeance. But this satanic enforcer of justice in a world where Revolution, like God, has failed, this demonic challenger of "global barbarism" by its own means, is Colley's creation. Andy may laugh when Colley tells him "you're not God", and insist that "Nobody is", but Colley is, in one respect, his Creator, since it is his arguments that have convinced Andy that "there is no feasible excuse for what we are, for what we have made of ourselves". When

Andy reels off the litany of the world's sins — "We have chosen to put profits before people, money before morality, dividends before decency, fanaticism before fairness, and our own trivial comforts before the unspeakable agony of others" (p. 301) — Colley recognises in them "something [he] once wrote". Colley's language has been his defense against his own fearfulness but through that language he has created his own antithesis, a fearful self by which the world is truly terrorized.

When Andy disappears at the end of the novel he leaves the terror behind. That is why, in the final chapter of the novel, Colley recollects how he, Andy and their girlfriends visited Mary King's Close, a street under the ground level of modern Edinburgh which was sealed off during the plague, its inhabitants trapped in their domestic tomb. The modern city was built over this time-capsule of the past and, like the many tourists who now visit it, their visit was "just for a laugh", part of the game of PR for the opening of a new branch of the *The Gadget Shop*. But in that underground world of the past, Colley experiences the roots from which humanity derives:

But in those moments of blackness you stood there, as though you yourself were made of stone like the stunted, buried buildings around you, and for all your educated cynicism, for all your late-twentieth-century materialist Western maleness and your fierce despisal of all things superstitious, you felt a touch of true and absolute terror, a consummately feral dread of the dark; a fear rooted back somewhere before your species had truly become human. . . . (p. 310)

Primordial fear is what happens when a modern "game" turns into ancient reality, or when ancient reality revisits itself upon the "games" of modern civilisation. It is that primordial world that the children first discover in the tunnel running through Andy's parents' estate, where they feel "that utter blackness . . . the cold, dead scent of the abandoned tunnel, rising up around you like some remorseless chilly breath" (p. 46). It is into the same tunnel that Andy and Colley pitch the body of their attacker. And it is the return to and the return of that primordial world that Colley will experience finally when he is Andy's prisoner: "I can hear the dead men, hear their flayed souls, wailing on the wind to no ear save mine and no understanding at all . . . dark going dark, black stinking hell o mum o dad o no no please don't take me back there" (p. 289).

Complicity ties Andy and Colley together as mutually defining fearful characters, but as so often in the modern novel, from Marlow and Kurtz in Joseph Conrad's *Heart of Darkness* to Nick Carraway and Jay Gatsby in F. Scott Fitzgerald's *The Great Gatsby*, one of the two paired characters goes beyond the bounds of ordinary experience, and one remains just within the boundary, able to see into the abyss but remaining behind to tell the tale of the other's unspeakable experience. Andy, fearless, has gone beyond the boundaries of the human community; his need, by the end, is simply to tell Colley why. Colley remains within, knowing that he has, in many ways, created the very force which terrorizes and diminishes him. At the novel's conclusion, Colley is nursing a cancer, the cancer that is Andy, like a growth within himself, just as Andy nurses Colley's words within himself as the justification of his own demented actions.

SEXUAL TRANSGRESSIONS

Immediately before their confrontation with the "policeman" who attempts who attempts to rape Andy, Colley is discussing with his friend their experience of girls, something he feels Andy's equal in because Colley "mixed with girls every day" in his local school whereas Andy was at an all-boys boarding school and "only really knew his sister Clare":

> "Have you ever seen Clare's?"
> "Don't be disgusting."
> "What's disgusting? She's your sister!"
> "Exactly."
> "What do you mean?"
> "You don't know anything, do you?" (p. 196)

The scene establishes Colley's innocence of the taboos that govern sexual relations, an innocence that leads him into masturbating Andy, whose erection is something he has no experience of. Working to Andy's instructions he produces an ejaculation which is equally novel to him — "Yuk. What a mess" — while Andy congratulates him on having done "not bad . . . For a beginner" (p. 198). The implication that Andy has developed a homoerotic inclination at his single sex school is emphasized at this point in the narrative by the fact that "his free hand went to my head, stroking my hair" (p. 197) but it has already been implied in an earlier (but chronologically later) scene when Colley phones Andy and is asked, "You ever go the other way these days?. . . . You know, with guys" (p. 75). Colley's amazement produces a "tone that sounds . . . at least disapproving if not actually homophobic", to which Andy responds that he "has lost interest in all that stuff", while also admitting that "old habits die hard".

The implication of continuing homosexual interests on Andy's part is apparently shocking to Colley, but again there seems to be a deep divide between Colley's conscious and his subconscious responses. Colley's only female lover in the book, Yvonne, is more "masculine" in terms of strength and fighting ability than Colley, as we see in their fight in Chapter 4. He refers to her initially only as

"Y", which not only negates her feminine name but suggests masculinity by the fact that the Y-chromosome is the male chromosome. Equally, she refers to him as "bitch-boy" (p. 132) and is unsatisfied by his sexual assault on her until he mounts her from the rear, as though in a homosexual coupling. A sexual preference for the masculine is also implied in William's greeting to Andy when he is first introduced, "So you're Cam's soldier boy" (p. 184). Colley's own behaviour points sometimes towards a repressed homoeroticism. Drunk after an evening with his friend Al he believes that flowers Al has bought are for him, and is confused when he is told they are for Andi, mistaking Al's wife's name for Andy's and making us aware of the Y that connects Yvonne to Andy. Drunk at Andy's hotel, Colley relates that

I put an arm round Andy's neck at one point and say, You know I love you, old buddy, and isn't friendship and love what's it's really all about? and why can't people just see that and just be *nice* to each other? except that there just so *many* complete bastards in the world, but Andy shakes his head and I try to kiss him. . . . (p. 146)

The "love" for Andy which can only express itself when Colley is drunk points back to fact that their childhood homoeroticism was pre-empted by the grotesque interruption of an adult sexuality, and points back to their homosexuality as suspended and unfulfilled rather than forgotten.

Colley believes that his betrayals of Andy are the two childhood moments when he ran away, but there is another crucial moment in their relationship, the moment when, as students, Yvonne leaves William's bed and comes to Colley's and makes love to him. Not realizing that Andy is also in the same room, in his sleeping bag, Yvonne tells Colley "This never happened". After she leaves,

I lift my head up and look down to the floor at the foot of the bed, where Andy is lying curled up in his sleeping bag, unseen in the shadows, which is why I was being quiet.

"Andy?" I whisper quietly, thinking that maybe he slept through it all.

"Lucky fucking bastard," he says in a normal voice.

I lie back, laughing silently. (p. 189)

The immediate meaning of the passage points to Andy's envy of Colley's "fucking", making him the "lucky . . . bastard". However, the word "lie" in this passage connects directly to Colley's narratorial lie, "I lied about something" (p. 183), which introduced this section of the novel, and what he has lied about is the fact that Andy does not know about his relationship with Yvonne: "I don't want Andy to know about me and Yvonne", he tells us, *as though* Andy has no knowledge of their relationship at all: "This is awkward because Andy knows Yvonne and William from our Stirling days; he used to be really friendly with William and, though they seem to have gone their separate ways, I don't want Andy to know about me and Yvonne" (p. 74). What the later acknowledgment of the "lie" reveals is that Andy has every reason to suspect that Colley's married lover is Yvonne: "Frightened I'll tell somebody?" Andy asks, and Colley replies, "Yeah. I live in perpetual fear our enormous circle of mutual friends will find out" (p. 75). Colley's irony reveals the truth: their very small circle of mutual friends could easily betray him, since Andy has possible reason to want retribution for Colley's betrayals of him.

The significance of Colley's narratorial lie to the readers and of his personal evasion with Andy is pointed up when Andy leaves the fingers of one of his final victims laid out in the window of a fishshop: "Andy had used the doc's fingers to spell out I LIED on the counter" (p. 268). To the police, this reads as Andy's acknowledgment of the fact that he had promised not to kill the doctor;

to us as readers of Colley's "I lied" it becomes a personal message to Colley himself, as he admits when "the idea of Andy paying a visit occurred to me as well, after that I LIED" (p. 268). Andy lied, but his admission matches Colley's: if Colley lied about his relationship with Yvonne, did Andy also lie when he said that "he has lost interest in all that stuff"? The connections between the narrative incidents reveals that when Colley "lie[s] back, laughing silently", he knows that more has been broken than just where he "can feel blood on my shoulder, where her teeth broke the skin" (p. 189). Andy's killing of William, despite the long litany of William's crimes against humanity, is insufficiently explained unless it is the deliberate effort to achieve vengeance against Yvonne for her usurpation of Andy's rights: " 'Taking advantage of you, Cameron,' she purrs" (p. 188) to which he responds, in Andy's hearing "I'm a man of easy virtue" (p. 189). Colley's easy relationship with a woman is a further betrayal that is acknowledged only indirectly by the lie—both to himself and to the reader—that attempts to conceal the significance of Andy's knowledge of his relationship with Yvonne.

Yvonne's "private" sex with Colley is in fact a public act: there is a third point of view—Andy's—from which it looks very different from the viewpoint of either of the immediate participants so that it is not only William who is threatened by their substitution of the rules of their own games for the accepted rules of marriage. The relation of point of view to rules is pointed up in the key piece of evidence which implicates Colley in the murders that Andy is carrying out. It is a business card from someone who works for *Jane's Defence Weekly*—a title which underlines, by combining a "feminine" name with the "masculine" business of war, the transfer of characteristics between the sexes—and on which Colley has written some of the keyboard instructions for the game of *Despot* with which he is obsessed. The first is "Ctr + Alt 0 = PoV chnge"

(p. 179), where PoV stands for "Point of View", and the importance
of "Point of View" is revealed through the game itself: "the tempta-
tion in *Despot* is always to swap PoV, which people who don't know
the game always think sounds sort of innocent, like some detail, but
it isn't: you're not just swapping Point of View, you're swapping
your current Despotic Power Level for something less" (pp. 133–4).
Each character has a point of view which gives them a "Despotic
Power Level" and what counts as transgression changes depending
on point of view. Andy and Colley's initial sexual encounter is
innocent from Colley's point of view, meaningful from Andy's, and
"dirty" from the point of view of the onlooking "policeman". Their
later relationship is one of "buddies" from Colley's point of view
but of betrayal from Andy's. Yvonne's relationship with Colley is a
betrayal of William but it is also a betrayal of Colley, whom she is
simply using for sexual gratification. William's relationship with all
three is based primarily on his desire for personal advancement, on
his desire to "take" as much as possible from all of them. When
Andy opens "The Gadget Shop", he attempts the stunt of filling a
pyramid of champagne glasses, "a champagne bottle in one hand
and his other arm held by William, who leans out the opposite way
to balance him" (p. 203). William is Andy's balance — on the opposite side of Yvonne he keeps Colley in place, in *play*, unable to
fulfil the heterosexual relationship which would finally exclude
Andy. For William, however, this is a purely financial calculation:

"William!" somebody yells from the crowd. "Fifty quid if you just let
him go!"

"Don't you fucking dare, Sorrell!" Andy shouts, laughing, up-ending the
magnum over the topmost glass as the bottle empties.

"Not for a measly fifty," William laughs, as he and Andy pull together
and draw together. . . . (p. 203)

The four of them are pulled together and drawn together in a series of mutual transgressions whose consequences will eventually destroy the balance which keeps them in play together.

SPELLING OUT THE TRUTH

As Colley drives back in to Edinburgh in Chapter 8 he notes that the typography of the new signs for the Euro-summit "makes *me* want to pronounce the word Edin-burg, and I *live* there for God's sake" (p. 175). The conflict of written and oral forms of the name is compounded on the following page: "Edin-burgh, Edin-borrow" (p. 176), as though the English language has "borrowed" and deformed them for its own purposes. The clash between ancient Scottish names and the country's dominant language — its dominant point of view — is comically pointed up by Colley's journalist colleague Frank, who delights in discovering how the spell-checker on his wordprocessor garbles Scottish places names: "Yetts o' Muckart becomes Yetis o' Muscat under the spell-check" (p. 18). The spell-check has transgressed on to territory it cannot understand. It cannot cast its "spell" over Scotland, which mocks its efforts to discover meaning, or opens up alternative, often threatening meanings. The name of the pub where Colley is asked to wait for a phonecall from Andy, *The Last Drop*, might be a model of language in *Complicity*, since its contemporary significance to pub drinkers — the last drop in the glass — conceals its grim historical reality — it is in the Grassmarket where criminals were taken for public hanging, a very final "last drop". The two meanings come together when it becomes the place where Andy indicates where he will "drop off" the last of his victims. Like the trapdoor on a gallows, language in *Complicity* drops us suddenly from one dimension of meaning into another.

We can trace such effects in the names of characters themselves, which hint at their roles in the narrative. Andy's surname is Gould, and he has indeed become the creator of horrors, has been "ghouled". In Scots, "to colley" means both to domineer and to give in, describing exactly Colley's double function, as he dominates his computer games but is subdued by reality. Colley's surname, however, is also suspiciously close both to the nickname of the newspaper he works for, the *Caley*—as though his role as a journalist has become a substitute for his real identity—but also to that of William Calley, the U.S. officer who was convicted of war crimes in Vietnam, and who is mentioned in Chapter 11 (p. 264). Calley's first name, of course, is shared with William, Yvonne's husband, whose surname, Sorrell, gestures both to "sorrel", the acid tasting plant ("salts of sorrel" is a very poisonous chemical) and to Sorel, the anarcho-syndicalist whose philosophy is often cited as one of the roots of Fascism. The names of the characters "spell" out the truths concealed behind their surface identities, as though, like the fact that Colley's editor is called Eddie—Eddie the Ed—the accidents of language and the accidents of reality have come to match one another. Cameron—whose past is as though on camera—will eventually re*collec*t his past.

Precisely the opposite effect is produced by the sign near Andy's hotel—"Strome Ferry—no ferry" (p. 137)—which underlines how language and reality can become unjointed from one another. Colley comments of the sign that "that just says it all", but as a name pointing only to an absence "Strome Ferry" actually fails to *say* anything at all, revealing a language no longer able to map reality. The importance of such plays of language within the novel is implied in the name of the place where the childhood traumas occurred—the Carse of Strath*speld*. Frank's spellcheck turns "Carse" into "Curse": it is a place which has been misspelled and Andy and Colley are trapped by the "spell" by which the events in

Strathspeld have cursed their lives. Breaking that "spell" requires a language capable of expressing—of *spell*ing out—what has happened. Despite the fact that he is journalist who is supposed to have power over language, it is precisely the inability to find a language for the horrors of life that defeats Colley when he goes to cover the war against Iraq.

> I gave it half and hour and still couldn't think of anything that would describe how it looked and how I felt. . . .
>
> The black, charred boot was a couple of metres away, half-buried in the sand. When I picked it up it was surprisingly heavy because it still had the foot inside it.
>
> I wrinkled my nose at the stink and let it drop, but it didn't help, didn't break the log-jam, didn't (ha) kick-start the process.
>
> Nothing did. (p. 292)

The detached foot, filling the boot rather than the boot protecting the foot, inverts the relationship between the human body and the things around it, an inversion which Colley can only express in the accidental puns of a joke—"kick-start the process"—because he is still caught in the deeper pun represented by the "log-jam" that was the killing in Strathspeld.

Colley's entrapment in the failure of language is mirrored in the false connections and false meanings of the "Ares" conspiracy: the name of the god of massacres points him to killings in the past but conceals from him the very real massacres going on in the present, murders related to the other murder in the past whose memory he has suppressed. While Colley is trapped in false languages that separate him from reality, Andy is engaged in bringing language and reality very directly back into contact with each other, since each of his killings is not simply an event, but a sign; his victims, like the fingers with which he spells out "I LIED", are turned into texts. Thus the editor is not just thrown out of a window, he is "spiked" like a journalist's story; the judge who is lenient to rapists is raped, the doctor who failed to diagnose Clare's illness is dissected and the officer who failed to lead his men effectively is stood on a plinth designed for a war memorial. The nature of the crimes committed by Andy's victims is *spelled* out by the manner of their deaths. The language which they deform in order to mask their crimes — "It was my judgement that the interest of the West would best be served if the Iran-Iraq War went on for as long as possible" (p. 58) — returns to take vengeance by transforming them into a language that advertises the truth they have tried to conceal. Through Andy's ghoulish inventions a world trapped in falsehood is redeemed: the truth needs the complicity of evil if it is to be able to speak itself.

FROZEN TIME

The narrative of *Complicity* works in a variety of different temporal modes. There is the time of reading, in which we are acquiring information in a certain order; there is the time of the events of 1992, which occur successively; there is the time of the recollection the past, which happens with changing emphases as we move towards Colley's recollection of his traumatically submerged memories, and there is another time, the time of myth, of the fable, which refuses to be incorporated into the successive order of ordinary temporality.

The novel is structured around a series of encounters with mythic time but a mythic time which does not redeem the world from the mere succession of ordinary temporality — as Christianity or Edwin Muir's "fable" claims to do — but reveals only its barren and wasted condition. When Colley is released from prison he discovers that his 'Tosh' has been left on and that the game of *Despot* has gone on playing, independently of him: "I can't believe its the same game. I feel my mouth open. It's a wasteland. My kingdom is gone" (p. 261). T. S. Eliot's *The Waste Land* (1922) is one of the major allusive contexts of Banks's fiction. It not only provides the titles of two of his science fiction works — *Consider Phlebas* and *Look to Windward* — it also provides much of the allusive context of *The Bridge*. Banks's novel is focused on the Forth Bridge just as Eliot's poem takes as one of its central symbols London Bridge: both are places where the protagonist must confront the world of the living dead — "A crowd flowed over London Bridge, so many, /I did not think death had undone so many" — and must journey across a mythic desert to recovery lost memory. In *The Bridge*, as in *The Waste Land*, the recovery of memory offers the possibility of escape from the "wasteland", but in *Complicity* Colley's recovery of memory is only the prelude to the further devastation that Andy wreaks upon the world, wasting the kingdom that they should have inherited.

In *Complicity* descent into the mythic, as in the descent into Mary King's Close, is not redemptive — it is the touch of death. This is why the primal scene of the narrative is Andy's apparent drowning under the ice. Andy is trapped for ten minutes in the freezing water after he has been abandoned by Colley and "while the doctor had heard about children, usually younger than Andy, surviving without air in cold water" he had "never seen anything like it" (p. 161). Andy's survival is miraculous — "It was a miracle, his mother said, and the local paper agreed" (p. 161) — but his icy resurrection does not bring knowledge of either eternity or redemption to come, but only knowledge of the frozen wasteland that is the modern world. Eliot's poem is built around the notion of the "fisher king" of ancient mythologies whose wound causes the land to be infertile. Andy's spilled semen that Colley brushes off on "the leaves and blades as I dash past" (p. 231) is the lost fertility that would have fertilized their land. Instead, in the years of the Cold War, Andy remains the "ice child" and Colley's seed is spilled in his infertile relationship with Yvonne, the ice with which she paints his penis a symbol of their sterile pleasure. After he has been shown the remains of Andy's victims, Colley has nightmares in which he is "stalked by a gorilla with the voice of a baby and a huge syringe and he wants to fuck you" (p. 182): the syringe is the one Andy filled with the sperm of rent boys and injected into the porn merchant, fertility turned to waste, the baby voice a mockery of reproduction. In the inversion of sexual roles that the wasted land produces, Andy describes the syringe as "a big mother" (p. 89).

The wasted land is made real, for Colley, on the Basra Road, in the aftermath of the Allied bombing of the trapped Iraqi forces, where he watches "the furious, screaming tower of flame" from a wrecked oil well, "a filthy hundred metre Cypress of fire" (p. 291). The natural world is transformed into a "mad waste" (p. 290) that consumes itself in fire, exactly as Andy, the ice-child, becomes the fire-god who burns down his own castle. Andy survives fire, however, just as he survived the ice, and rises again out of the incinerated body he has left behind, whereas Colley consumes fire through his endless cigarettes, charring his insides until he is as sick as the world he is witness to. Resurrection, in *Complicity*, is not a miracle that brings the Prince of Peace but only a prelude to the resumption of the work of the god a massacres, Ares. In the fish shop window (the "fish" referring us both to the Fisher King and to the fish that was the symbol of early Christianity) are displayed the dissected remains of Dr. Halziell:

On the slab there are bits of meat, not fish. I recognise liver—ruddy chocolate brown and silky looking—kidneys like dark, grotesque mushrooms, what is probably a heart and various other cuts of meat, in steaks, cubes and strips. At top centre there is a large brain, creamy-grey-looking.

"Good Christ," McDunn whispers. Funny, it's that that brings the shivers. . . . (p. 265)

Christ's resurrection has been reversed: the world is in thrall to a god whose purpose is to turn spirit into body, to reduce life to its mechanical components, and to spread sterility from the deep, cold underworld—the tunnel that contains the body, the buried close under Edinburgh streets—through the vivid overground of natural fertility. What that god preaches is "a functional indifference more horrifying than evil" (p. 310), the indifference that comes from realizing that human beings have no purpose. Andy demands to know "Why are people so fucking *useless?*" (p. 213). What he means is why are they so incompetent but what appalls him is precisely their *uselessness*; it is their lack of purpose that makes him despair. He has already visited the afterlife under the ice and knows that nothing will justify human existence or bring justice for his losses. His gorilla mask reveals the evolutionary scheme which defines the only "use" of life—"the curse of Gorily" as Frank's spellchecker puts it. This degradation of the value of humanity to mere evolutionary process has not been resisted by the world he inhabits but has been adopted by it as its very justification: for William "greed is good" because "it's natural", "it's evolution" (p. 220). Colley's surrogate religion of addiction teaches him to value only "what really works", but his final statement of that "catechism" turns itself into a question about the source of fertility—"What fucking works?" (p. 48). In his case, no fucking works, in the sense of being regenerative. Held in bondage to the past, his kingdom is the wasted land, given life neither by evolutionary nor spiritual purposes, its boundaries guarded by the destructive forces of fire and ice.

The Novel's Reception and Performance

Complicity was first published in 1993, was No. 1 in the British Bestsellers List for three weeks, appeared as paperback in 1994 and went through six reprintings by 1996. It has been re-printed every year since. Reviews of the book in Britain were shaped primarily by the sense of Banks's development since *The Wasp Factory*: many reviews refer back to the first novel or to *The Bridge* to emphasize Banks's much more political use of the violence for which *The Wasp Factory* had made him famous and the "verve and pace" of the plotting as compared with *The Bridge*. The generic switch to detective novel-thriller is located as part of Banks's developing skills with the novel form, as is "the adroitness" of his splicing of past and present.

American reviews had no such perspective in which to place Banks's works since the "serious" novels — as opposed to the science fiction — had not been published in the United States of America, largely in the belief that their Scottish content would not appeal to readers. The emphasis, therefore, was on *Complicity*'s ingenuity, the fact that it was "irresistibly compelling", and there were efforts to place it in familiar generic contexts such as the political thriller or the novel about serial killers. The difference in Banks's reputation on each side of the Atlantic can be guaged from the fact that in a BBC poll to find who people thought were the greatest writers of the millennium, Banks was rated fifth (behind Shakespeare, Jane Austen, and, of modern writers, George Orwell but ahead of Dostoevsky and James Joyce); Banks himself noted that he probably would not make the top 500 in a similar poll in the United States of America. Rights for translations of *Complicity* have, however, been sold for almost all European languages and a Japanese edition was published in 1996.

Critical reception of Banks' non-science fiction works falls into three main categories.

1) Scottish criticism: Banks appears not only accounts of contemporary Scottish fiction — such as Thom Nairn's 'Iain Banks and the Fiction Factory', in *Scottish Fiction since the Seventies* (1993), but has begun to figure in histories of Scottish literature with a much longer perspective, such as Marshall Walker's *Scottish Literature since 1707* (1996). The emphasis in such accounts is to place Banks within the traditions of Scottish fiction and to see him as one of those Scottish writers — like Irvine Welsh and Alan Warner — who have successfully harnessed a 'generational' fiction to a new vision of Scottish society.

2) gender and psychoanalytic criticism: Banks' novels have been used by critics — such as Dietrich Schoene in *Writing Men: Literary Masculinities from Frankenstein to the New Man* (2000) — wishing to explore the nature of gender, and particularly of masculinity, and its representation in fiction. This is a mode of approach that often involves the development of psychoanalytic readings of the texts.

3) genre criticism: Banks' writings have begun to appear in studies of particular genres of writing, such as Victor Sage and Allan Lloyd Smith's *Modern Gothic: A Reader* (1996) and Scott McCracken's *Pulp: Reading Popular Fiction* (1998).

The Novel on Film

Complicity was made into a film which was released in 2000. It followed the very successful 1996 BBC television adaptation of *The Crow Road* in four episodes, and on the string of highly successful Scottish films—*Shallow Grave, Trainspotting,* not to mention *Braveheart*—which had made international stars out of actors such as Ewan MacGregor and Robert Carlyle. *The Crow Road* was directed by Gavin Millar, a veteran Scottish director almost of all of whose work had been done in England, much of it for the BBC, and it achieved record ratings and won a series of major awards, including "best programme of the year" at the Independent TV awards. The script for *The Crow Road* was done by Brian Elsley, and Millar and Elsley combined again to do the screen version of *Complicity*, with Johnny Lee Miller, who had played Sick Boy in *Trainspotting,* in the lead role. Despite its strong cast, including a very effective Brian Cox as the detective, McDunn, and despite the fact that it made a notable impact when it was released in Scotland, achieving audiences which, on the UK-wide basis, would have put it in the year's top ten films, the reviews of the film were disappointing and it never gained national screening. Indeed, it was one of the first films produced with the assistance of the Scottish Arts Council's film funding from the National Lottery and one of many which failed to achieve either financial or critical success, leading to a great deal of argument about the role of public funding for film in Scotland.

The general consensus was that *Complicity* had more the feel of a low budget television movie — like the more recent versions of Ian Rankin's Rebus novels, with John Hannah in the lead role — than a production for the big screen. While its "drugs and sex" theme might seem attractive to the audience that had responded to *Trainspotting*, its thriller format had to compete with the much slicker versions of that genre being produced by Hollywood from novels such as John Grisham's. What was one of its prime virtues in a Scottish context — that it did not try to sell its Scottishness but took it for granted — was probably also a factor in making it less appealing to an international audience.

The film, however, perhaps has inherent weaknesses that are attributable to the very complexity of Banks's plot, since the effect of the "double", which is tantalizing in the novel, never has the same intensity in the film — the camera's inability to mimic the switches between "you" and "I" in Banks's narrative means that we are never in any real doubt that Colley is not guilty of the murders attributed to him. Disentangling the conspiracy and clearing himself from the suspicions of the police is what the film's narrative is about — not escaping from the possibility that he is himself an amnesiac killer. Without that dimension of possible double identity that makes Colley a possible Jekyll and Hyde, the repression of childhood experience cannot operate as a parallel to contemporary events. The consequence is that the interconnections between Colley and Andy which are established in the novel in order to reveal Colley's *complicity* with Andy's crimes disappear. Colley is simply the dupe of a plot for revenge over a childhood failing rather than someone who has created the very creature by which he is stalked; he is someone unfairly trapped for a past error than someone who is deeply bound to the "other self" whose actions are being attributed to him.

The lack of adequate motivation in Andy's actions in the film derive from the fact that the double betrayal in childhood becomes a single betrayal only—the scene of Andy's falling through the ice disappears, leaving only the scene of the attack on the boys when they are adolescents. The film, in effect, undoes Banks's combination of the political thriller with a narrative of personal discovery by reducing the personal dimension till it fails to have any significant role in the narrative. Colley's *amnesia*, which Banks's narrative is designed to reveal as crucial to his character, is turned inside out— what is revealed in the flash forwards to the woods in which the attack on the boys took place is Colley's shared memory with Andy, rather than the fact that one remembers and one forgets. And the flashbacks to their student days and to the beginnings of Andy's business explain Andy's disillusionment but not the reasons for Colley's addictive personality. The film presents plenty of evidence of Colley's addiction but fails to find a means of dramatizing what the first person narration of novel provides: the sense of Colley's life as a constant flight from reality, a flight from reality which makes him gullible to the conspiracy theory that Andy weaves.

The loss of Colley's first betrayal and the near-drowning in the ice also undermines the significance of the "ice" imagery which is so prevalent in the novel and still appears in the film in Colley's sexual bondage episode with Yvonne. In the novel, the "ice child" is symbolically present as Yvonne sucks Colley with a mouthful of ice; in the film, no such connection can be made. The disappearance of the near-drowning also removes Andy from the condition of having been miraculously resurrected, of being one who has already crossed the boundary between life and death, reality and myth, and therefore of having become, in some sense, a supernatural creature, an elemental figure of vengeance rather than an accidental one.

Other elisions are equally crucial: the political focus of the novel has been reduced by making it less historically specific. Although Andy's role in the Falklands War remains, the doubling of it in Colley's experiences in the Desert Storm campaign disappears. Colley's crucial third moment of trauma, the moment when he is unable to make language relate to the horrors of the Basra Road, is removed. Since this is one of the key moments that connects the private world of childhood and the public world of war, the interaction between these two dimensions of the novel is lost in the film. Despite the scene where Andy comments on the fact that Argentinian mines in the Falklands had been made in Britain, his campaign is presented as though it were a personal vendetta, rather than the desperate carrying through of the revolution which Colley's socialism has failed to achieve.

The public-private dimensions of the narrative are shaped in the novel's opening by scene of protest against nuclear submarines. In the film this is translated into a "green" protest against nuclear dumping: the military, economic, and sexual significance of the "long, grossly phallic shape" of the submarine that "slide[s] into the narrows" has been excised and with it the suggestion of repressed homoeroticism as a source of the novel's action. Rather than the masturbatory activity in which the boys are engaged in the novel, the sexual context of the assault on them is reduced to a brief comment by Andy about whether Colley wants to "see it". Indeed, the film is insistently heterosexual in its presentation of relationships, making no use of Colley's drunken attempt to kiss Andy or Andy's use of a vibrator on one of his victims, or the question posed to Andy by that victim, "Closet queer, are you?" Indeed, the film's synopsis makes it clear that the youthful Andy is to show that he is attracted to Yvonne. There is no doubt that the homoerotic is a potentially disturbing aspect of Banks's plot—disturbing because it might imply a "politically incorrect" reading of the relationship of violence to repressed homosexuality. Indeed, Scott McCracken's study of popular fiction, *Pulp*, offers such a reading of the novel *Complicity* only to withdraw it. In a Freudian interpretation, McCracken suggests, *Complicity* is a version of the "masculine gothic" which

> reveals the transgressive desires that lie beneath the masquerade of "normal" masculinity. In this reading, hiding the body can be read as a repression of Andy and Cameron's "queer" desires, which have been externalised and made monstrous in their attacker. The act of hiding binds their friendship making each the other's double so that Cameron is always complicit with Andy's aggression. In such an interpretation, Andy's violent career would represent a return of their repressed mutual attraction. (p. 146)

He immediately negates this reading, however, by suggesting that it "reproduces a narrow and stereotyped version of same-sex relationships; it is too narrow in its understanding of horror's monstrous productivity". The film avoids the difficulties that such Freudian readings produce by the Freudian tactic of totally repressing it.

What the film does do, however, is substantially to rewrite the role of Clare, Andy's sister, to be a mirror-image of Colley in her drug addiction. The scene in which Andy fills a pyramid of champagne glasses at the opening of the Gadget Shop—which, in the film, is renamed "Icon"—is translated from one in which the glasses simply collapse under the weight of champagne to one in which Clare deliberately brings the structure crashing down by lifting a champagne glass out from the bottom. The potential self-destructiveness of Colley's addictions are fulfilled in Clare, making her his "double" more than Andy is, despite the fact that when Clare dies, in the novel, she has returned to Strathspeld with her "latest fiancé", has "given up doing coke and taken up healthy shit like running and swimming" (p. 208).

Perhaps the most intriguing decision of the makers of the film was their decision not to use popular music for the soundtrack. Colley surrounds himself with music constantly in the early scenes of the novel and Banks gives him very detailed musical accompaniments to his journeys. Popular music would, of course, have given the film a historical setting, potentially dating it, but its lack reduces yet further the interaction between Colley and the "public" world that he inhabits and the "private" worlds he tries to escape to. The significance of the word "private" is also reshaped by the film, since it is the boy's attacker who tells them that they are "on private land", while in the novel it is Andy who declares that his attacker has trespassed on to "private property". The significance of the "privacy" of Colley's first sexual experience that is suddenly turned into a public spectacle is reversed by the film, with the boys' sexual conversation being presented as an intrusion into someone else's private property.

The undoubtedly fine performances by some of the actors in the film, and the undoubted power of individual scenes in Banks's narrative, do not salvage it from being, fundamentally, a failure to translate the literary complexity of *Complicity* into an equivalent filmic complexity. Banks is a writer who subverts genres, plays games with forms, challenges our understanding of characters by linking them together not just by narrative but by images whose significance develops, like the images in a modernist poem, by their sudden juxtaposition of disparate contexts of meaning. There can be no place in the film for the scene in Mary King's Close because the imagery of the underground world, of fear, of the collapse of civilization—the imagery which gives depth and resonance to Banks's writing—has not been developed sufficiently for it to be significant.

Further Reading and Discussion Questions

FURTHER READING

Works of Iain Banks

Iain Banks has published the following 'serious' novels:

The Wasp Factory (1984)
Walking on Glass (1985)
The Bridge (1986)
Espedair Street (1987)
Canal Dreams (1989)
The Crow Road (1992)
Complicity (1993)
Whit (1995)
A Song of Stone (1997)
The Business (1999)

He has also published, as Iain M. Banks, the following science
fiction novels. The "M."—for "Menzies", pronounced "Mingiss", a
family name—was originally a publishing accident: he had in-
tended all his novels to be by Iain M. Banks but Macmillan, the
publishers of *The Wasp Factory*, thought plain Iain Banks was better. He reverted to "Iain M." for *Consider Phlebas*, his first science
fiction novel, and the distinction of genres by name became part of
the promotion of his work.

Consider Phlebas (1987)

The Player of Games (1988)

Use of Weapons (1990)

Against a Dark Background (1993)

Feersum Endjinn (1994)

Excession (1996)

Inversions (1998)

Look to Windward (2000)

A collection of Short Fiction under the name Iain M. Banks is

The State of the Art (1991)

(Auto)biographies

Banks's own version of his "autobiography" can be found at

http://books.guardian.co.uk/links/sites_on_writers/a-b/

Other biographies are available at

http://www.jthin.co.uk/banks1.htm
   [The James Thin bookshop]

www.slainte.org.uk/scotwrit/Authors/
[a database of Scottish authors]

There is also a considerable amount of information in the Iain Banks Fanzine *The Culture*, which can obtained from The Culture, 6 Caistor Close, Chorlton, Manchester, M16 8NW, and which now also has an informative website with links to lots of other Iain Banks (and Iain M. Banks) material at

http://members.nbci.com/TheCulture/

Criticism of Banks's Fiction

There is no full scale critical work on Banks's writings so far. Listings of criticism of Banks's work as they appear will be found in the Bibliography of Scotland maintained by the National Library of Scotland, and accessible at *http: /sbo.nls.uk/*

The following are the most substantial criticisms to date:

Ronald Binns, "Castles, books, and bridges: Mervyn Peake and Iain Banks". *Peake Studies*, vol. 2, no. 1 (Winter 1990)
[on *The Bridge* and *Walking on Glass* and their relationship to *Gormenghast*]

R. J. Lyall. "Postmodernist Otherworld: Postcalvinist Purgatory: an approach to *Lanark* and *The Bridge*." *Etudes Ecossaises*. 2, 1993, pp. 41–52.
[attempt to situate Banks and Alasdair Gray to a Scottish postmodernism]

Scott McCracken. *Pulp: Reading Popular Fiction.* (Manchester: Manchester Univ Press, 1998)
[A sustained reading of *Complicity*, pp. 144–50]

Tim Middleton. *Iain Banks* in Merritt Moseley (ed.), *British Novelists Since the 1960s*. (Detroit: Gale Research, 1998), pp. 19–27.

> [Substantially biographical but with brief critical commentary on the novels]

Tim Middleton. "Constructing the Contemporary Self: The Works of Iain Banks" in Tracey Hill and William Hughes (eds.), *Contemporary Writing and National Identity*. (Bath: Sulis Press, 1995).

> [argues for Banks's exploraton of the fragmented postmodern self]

Thom Nairn. "Iain Banks and the Fiction Factory", in Gavin Wallace and Randall Stevenson (eds), *Scottish Fiction Since the Seventies*. (Edinburgh: Edinburgh University Press, 1993), pp. 127–35.

> [A study of the early fiction in its Scottish context]

Dietrich Schoene. *Writing Men: Literary Masculinities from Frankenstein to the New Man*. (Edinburgh: Edinburgh University Press, 2000).

> [An analysis of the presentation of sexuality and gender in *The Wasp Factory*]

Richard Todd. *Consuming Fictions*. (London: Bloomsbury, 1996), pp. 148–156.

> [argues that *Complicity* upholds "the now conventional idea of postmodernist self-reflexiveness' but "gives it a new twist by suggesting that the real complicity is between those who connive at society's ills not simply by allowing them to happen, but by reading about them in — and writing about them for — the media"]

Victor Sage. "The Politics of Petrification: Culture, religion, history in the fiction of Iain Banks and John Banville". Victor Sage and Allan Lloyd Smith (eds.), *Modern Gothic: A Reader*. (Manchester: Manchester University Press, 1996).

> [argues that "the action of his books . . . tends to revolve around, or to end up in, a decaying feudal/imperial structure in which the future is being decided" and that "men are either converted to the female in themselves . . . or they belong to an (apparently) historically outmoded barabarian, male, warrior-culture"]

Marshall Walker. *Scottish Literature Since 1707* (London: Longman, 1996), pp. 342–6.
  [review of Banks's fiction in the context of contemporary Scottish writing]

Interviews

There have been many interviews with Iain Banks, and several useful ones are available on the Web, particularly at

www.books.guardian.co.uk/links/sites_on_writers
  [Guardian links]

http://freespace.virgin.net/questing.beast/scrawl_feature4.htm
  [Interview originally in *Scrawl*]

http://www.sandm.co.uk/sfjournm/Iain_Banks/body_iain_banks.html
  [Science Fiction Journal]

Early interviews which cast light on Banks's development and Scottish interests include,

Kate Kelman. "A Collision of Selves". *Cencrastus*, 60, 1998, pp. 19–22.
James Robertson. "Bridging Styles. *Radical Scotland*. 42, Dec. 1989, pp. 26–7.
Richard Tallaron. "Iain Banks". *Etudes Ecossaises*, 3, 1996, pp. 141–8.

Scottish Context

Cairns Craig (ed.). *The History of Scottish Literature: Volume Four: Twentieth Century*. (Aberdeen: University of Aberdeen Press, 1987).
Cairns Craig. *The Modern Scottish Novel: Narrative and the National Imagination*. (Edinburgh: Edinburgh University Press, 1999).
George Davie. *The Democratic Intellect*. (Edinburgh: Edinburgh University Press, 1961).

George Davie. *The Crisis of the Democratic Intellect*. (Edinburgh: Polygon, 1986).

Tom Devine. *The Scottish Nation*. (London: Penguin, 1999).

Francis Hart. *The Scottish Novel*. (London: John Murray, 1979).

DISCUSSION QUESTIONS

Characters

- On a website a fan described Colley as "cool": to what extent does the novel make Colley the moral "hero" of the narrative?

- Trace the ways in which aspects of Andy's experience and personality are repeated in Colley, William and Yvonne.

- Analyze the role of Clare in the narrative.

- "[He] held a hand out to me. I put my hand up to his. I remembered William and Andy, balanced on the chair under the old hovercraft" (p. 215). Consider the ways in which the central characters "balance" one another.

- To what extent are Banks's characters fixed in their personalities from the beginning of the narrative and to what extent do they develop through the novel?

- Consider the characterisation of the minor characters and how they relate to the themes of the novel as a whole.

Events

- Discuss the relationship between the sexual games that Colley and Yvonne play and the general themes of the novel (consider, for instance, the implications of "bonds").

- Analyze the possible double meanings in the characters' comments during the card game on p. 283; which game are they talking about when they ask for cards?
- Consider the significance of the different disguises used by the "you" during the various killings.
- What is the purpose of the story about Scotch whisky in the "Chill Filter" chapter?
- Consider the significance of travel in the novel.
- Why does Banks make William the inheritor of land in the Scottish Highlands and of an island that is a graveyard?
- What is the purpose of the conflict between the locals and the travellers at Stromeferry?

Structures

- Analyze the time shifts of Chapter 8: what is the significance of the order in which incidents are narrated?
- Examine the different ways in which the self-addressing "you" is used throughout the narrative.
- What is the significance of the chapter titles in relation to the content of each of the chapters?
- Analyze the different status given to past events in terms of direct narration, recollection and recovery of lost memories.
- "There is only one suspect left and that's me" (p. 221); how effective is Banks's narration in maintaining our sense of who might be innocent, who guilty?

Images and Symbols

- Analyze the symbolic significance of the various computer games that Colley plays.

- Trace the significance of "boots" in the novel.
- "She goes suddenly very still, whispering "Baby, baby" to me" (p. 95): analyze the significance of the "baby" imagery in the novel.
- Analyze the imagery of pp. 286–288 and connect it with the imagery of the rest of the novel.

Issues

- "This is purely coincidence, of course; it's not fate, not karma, not anything except a fortuitous accident" (p. 52). Consider the relationship between fate and accident in the novel.
- "With this act of treachery I can finally buy my freedom from the burden of buried horror" (p. 235). Discuss the relationship between treachery and purchase ("buy") in the novel.
- To what extent does the novel make us, as readers, complicit in the crimes committed?
- What is the significance of the fact that Andy is not caught at the end of the novel and is helped to escape by Colley?
- Is this a novel which can be read only once because it can no longer hold the reader's attention when we know who the murderer is?
- To what extent is Andy a "justified sinner"?